Lavender Fields

THE FEMINIST WIRE BOOKS
Connecting Feminisms, Race, and Social Justice

SERIES EDITORS
Monica J. Casper, Tamura A. Lomax, and Darnell L. Moore

EDITORIAL BOARD
Brittney Cooper, Aimee Cox, Keri Day, Suzanne Dovi, Stephanie Gilmore, Kiese Laymon, David J. Leonard, Heidi R. Lewis, Nakisha Lewis, Adela C. Licona, Jeffrey Q. McCune Jr., Joseph Osmundson, Aishah Shahidah Simmons, Stephanie Troutman, Heather M. Turcotte

ALSO IN THE FEMINIST WIRE BOOKS
A Love Letter to This Bridge Called My Back, edited by gloria j. wilson, Joni B. Acuff, and Amelia M. Kraehe

Black Girl Magic Beyond the Hashtag: Twenty-First-Century Acts of Self-Definition, edited by Julia S. Jordan-Zachery and Duchess Harris

The Chicana Motherwork Anthology, edited by Cecilia Caballero, Yvette Martinez-Vu, Judith C. Pérez-Torres, Michelle Téllez, and Christine Vega

Them Goon Rules: Fugitive Essays on Radical Black Feminism, by Marquis Bey

LAVENDER FIELDS

Black Women Experiencing
Fear, Agency, and Hope
in the Time of COVID-19

Edited by JULIA S. JORDAN-ZACHERY

THE UNIVERSITY OF
ARIZONA PRESS

TUCSON

The University of Arizona Press
www.uapress.arizona.edu

We respectfully acknowledge the University of Arizona is on the land and territories of Indigenous peoples. Today, Arizona is home to twenty-two federally recognized tribes, with Tucson being home to the O'odham and the Yaqui. Committed to diversity and inclusion, the University strives to build sustainable relationships with sovereign Native Nations and Indigenous communities through education offerings, partnerships, and community service.

ISBN-13: 978-0-8165-4736-4 (paperback)
ISBN-13: 978-0-8165-4737-1 (e-book)

Cover design by Leigh McDonald
Title font Millimetre by Jérémy Landes (Velvetyne Type Foundry)
Interior designed and typeset by Sara Thaxton in 10.25/15 Minion Pro with Millimetre, Berling LT Std, and Helvetica LT Std

Publication of this book is made possible in part by support from the Wake Forest College of Arts and Sciences.

Library of Congress Cataloging-in-Publication Data
Names: Jordan-Zachery, Julia S., 1971– editor.
Title: Lavender fields : Black women experiencing fear, agency, and hope in the time of COVID-19 / edited by Julia S. Jordan-Zachery.
Other titles: Feminist wire books.
Description: Tucson : The University of Arizona Press, 2023. | Series: The feminist wire books, connecting feminisms, race, and social justice | Includes bibliographical references and index.
Identifiers: LCCN 2022014572 (print) | LCCN 2022014573 (ebook) | ISBN 9780816547364 (paperback) | ISBN 9780816547371 (ebook)
Subjects: LCSH: African American women—Social conditions. | COVID-19 Pandemic, 2020—Personal narratives. | COVID-19 (Disease)—Psychological aspects. | LCGFT: Personal narratives.
Classification: LCC E185.86 .L378 2023 (print) | LCC E185.86 (ebook) | DDC 305.48/89607309052—dc23/eng/20220608
LC record available at https://lccn.loc.gov/2022014572
LC ebook record available at https://lccn.loc.gov/2022014573

Printed in the United States of America
♾ This paper meets the requirements of ANSI/NISO Z39.48-1992 (Permanence of Paper).

CONTENTS

ACKNOWLEDGMENTS

When the ancestors call, *I often say my job is to listen.* I tried not to listen to the call for this project; the work seemed too much. Yet the ancestors did not walk away. And for that, I am grateful. I am also thankful for my Black women's writing group: Angela Lewis, Deidre Flowers, Leta Hopper, Danielle Cooper, and Courtney Buggs. Thanks to Michelle Meggs and Celeste Henery and Wendy Grossman—you all were always in my corner, encouraging me when I thought that I could not do it. To the reviewers, much gratitude for seeing this project and, more importantly, for seeing Black women. To my mother, Monica Jordan, and my grandmother, Kathleen Griffith, thank you for always being in my corner. Thanks, dad, Evan Jordan, for allowing me to dream. Makeen Zachery, you are always asking, "You need help?" and I thank you for that. Finally, thanks to all the contributors for the trust you've given me with your words and for the beautiful community we have formed.

Lavender Fields

Toward a Knotless Back

My
masseuse
says my back
is tight. Hubby
agrees. Therapist
asks what my rituals
are these days. If I put the
out-of-office reply on, though
we're all out of the office, then I
shouldn't peek at my work email at all.
Then maybe I'll remember not to hold
my breath, not to grind my teeth at night.
Will stretch first thing in the morning
Do they call it child's pose cause
it makes my daughter smile?
Work is not on her
mind and not mine.
We break/fast—
Start our
day.

—*LeConté J. Dill*

When Will the COVID Be Over?

Julia S. Jordan-Zachery

Who knows? Maybe you were made queen for just such a time as this.

—Esther 4:14, *New Message Bible*

No hour is ever eternity, but it has its right to weep.

—Zora Neale Hurston, *Their Eyes Were Watching God*

Her face, as she prepares the Art that is her gift, is a legacy of respect she leaves
to me, for all that illuminates and cherishes life. She has handed down her
respect for the possibilities—and the will to grasp them.

—Alice Walker, *In Search of Our Mothers' Garden*

Our Testimonies

Black women, whispering in the midnight hour,
Mama on her knees uttering a prayer,
gently touching our shoulders as they share a word of wisdom,
shaping us,
preparing us,
to birth the work we were sent on earth to do.

Sometimes, it comes to us in the air,
a gentle whisper, or
a loud bang
what feels like an accidental meeting,

Is the ancestors, who have a way about them?

We know, Black women have a way of knowing.

I start this book on African/Black women's testimonies of living with COVID-19 by situating myself and my role in it.

Over my twenty-plus years as an academician, I have evolved. I started simply wanting to be a political scientist who focused on Black women and public policy. I saw my work as an extension of me, but not in the way I do at this stage of my career. There was a shift in my approach to being an academician at some point. I started journaling about being a storyteller of Black women's stories. Research, what I had been trained in, took a back seat, and the notion of storytelling became more prominent. I cannot explain this shift, and I have learned that some things need not be explained over time. Sometimes, Black women simply know (see Hill Collins 2000).

Then COVID-19 hit.

At some point during shelter in place—I have lost count of how long I have been at home—the Black feminine ancestors whispered to me. They called on me to undertake this project on Black women and COVID-19. I resisted. The project felt too big for me. I was worried that I could not do it and do it well.

I went out into my garden. The energy of the ancestors deepened, and the call seemed to wrap itself around me in a way that would not release me. I did not feel threatened. But I resisted. I stayed in my garden for hours in my efforts to resist—weeding, tending, and avoiding. Finally, the heat of the day caught up to me, and I slowly made my way inside. I needed to find something else to occupy my mind, something that allowed me to continue avoiding the call for this project.

But you said you wanted to be a storyteller. You wanted to tell the stories of Black women. I heard it, and it was whispered to me without judgment, like my grandmother giving me a gentle reminder to be safe when I left the house. A reminder of what I had written time and time again in my journal, as I contemplated how I wanted to be as a Black woman, an academic, the ancestors spoke. *A storyteller. A teller of Black women's stories.* I lingered at the door. I took my hat off and slipped into my "house shoes." The ancestors were patient. They knew—just like Black women have a way of knowing, they knew— that this project was birthed.

After entering the house, I cannot recall much more other than glancing up from my computer with a call for papers drafted. Never have I written in this manner before. I do not remember pausing to think about words—it was effortless. My gran would often tell us, "What's for you is for you." I called her, just to hear her voice. I knew that she would help me make sense of what I had just experienced. How could I have written this call and cannot remember the process of thinking about it?

And then I remembered that I also wrote in my journals—I will only tell the stories given to me. *Lavender Fields* is a story, an African/ African Diaspora/Black woman's story, that was given to me. It is a story about the I and the we, as the lines between our individual and collective survival are often blurred. I am the vessel through which these testimonies are offered. But it is not my story. And so, I am careful as to how I tell it.

We have so few accounts of Black women's experiences with the Spanish flu of 1918–19. But we know that there are stories that linger like the one I share about my mother and her young neighbor below. And while we may not know these stories in the way Western philosophic thought suggests that knowing happens, as Black women, we know. As Black women, we feel Black women's experiences with the Spanish flu in our bones. While we know, we also recognize what it means for these women's stories not to have been recorded. The silence of their stories speaks to how Black women are at times made hypervisible yet invisible (see Jordan-Zachery 2017; Dickens, Womack, and Dimes 2019). We are often relegated to a footnote, if that. To ensure that our experiences are captured, I organized a series on Black women and COVID-19. *Lavender Fields* is part of this series. *Black Women and da Rona: Community, Consciousness, and Ethics of Care* completes the series. Through autoethnography, *Lavender Fields* takes up the stories of African/African Diaspora/Black girls and women living through and with COVID-19.

As Aisha Durham (2017, 23) tells us, "Autoethnography is a spiritual act of political self-determination, of reclamation." By centering themselves and African/African Diaspora/Black girls and women in relation to society, the authors of these essays and reflections make real our fears, hopes, and desires. This is a raw telling of African/African Diaspora/Black girls' and women's experiences, written in real time and as some of the contributors battled COVID-19 themselves. This type of writing is not the same as writing "post," where time offers a different lens and a distance. As I thought through how to honor these stories, I found myself drawn to how Alice Walker (1975) honors Zora Neale Hurston. As such, I use Walker as a template for engaging the essays and thought pieces of *Lavender Fields*.

In line with Black feminist works (see Jordan-Zachery and Harris 2019; Boylorn 2016; Combahee River Collective 2014; Allen 2009; Hill Collins 2000; hooks 1989), the essays and thought pieces center Black girls and women and their testimonies in hopes of moving them from the margin to the center (hooks 1984). Furthermore, by centering the stories of Black girls' and women's experiences with COVID-19, *Lavender Fields* is justice and equity oriented.

There is much to unearth in this text, and I want to bring a bit of a spotlight to the approach (I use that term with caution). I rely on Alice Walker, particularly her search for Zora Neale Hurston, to situate the testimonies offered here. In her tale of finding Hurston, Walker offers a technique of engaging in testimony. I tease out that technique by centering four elements: markers, the in-between space of knowing–unknowing–not knowing, community/lineage, and desires. Before I explore this technique (by placing Walker's words alongside the contributors' words), I first offer a snapshot of African/African Diaspora/Black women's experiences with COVID-19. This snapshot is focused primarily on the scant data that speak to women, as girls seem nonexistent in the data collection on COVID-19.

When Will the COVID Be Over?

"When will the COVID be over? I wish the COVID was over!" she cried in the way only a five-year-old could—full of passion and truth. She stood outside of the gate like she does every day on her way home from school. Except that today COVID had disrupted their routine.

One could hear the ringing bell from the back patio, signaling the end of the school day. In a few minutes, she knew that her doorbell would ring. This was their Monday through Friday routine. And so, she shifted and got herself ready to greet her weekday visitor. Like clockwork, her bell rang. Her hand was poised on the doorknob as she heard the chime. Standing on the other side of the gate was her little five-year-old visitor. The friendship between these two, one five and the other seventy-four, was one to behold. They often sat on the bench in the garage discussing their days, the five-year-old sharing songs and teaching the elder all that she had learned that day at school. They both sat on a bench that had heard so many stories over its fifty years, separated by age, yet close in their delight of marveling at the school day. But on this day, the routine was ruptured. COVID.

The five-year-old patiently waited for her elder (her neighbor) to open the gate. Each stood looking at the other. Finally, the little girl's grandmother, standing nearby, told her, "You know you can't hug Mrs. Jordan," to which the little girl passionately declared, "When will the COVID be over?! I want the COVID to be over!" Tears flowed down her little upturned face. My mother, Mrs. Jordan, stared forlornly at her little neighbor, who had become a part of her daily routine. Both lives disrupted and with no end in sight.

Like my mother's five-year-old neighbor, as we see the "second," "third," and possibly "fourth" wave of the pandemic COVID-19, also referred to as da 'Rona, many of us ask, "When will the COVID be over?" In the United States, 622,845 lives had been lost as of July 2021. In Barbados, where my mother resides, forty-eight lives had been lost by that same time (WorldOMeter, n.d.). I "sit" in both places. Black women and girls in the United States are among the hardest hit by COVID-19 in terms of illnesses, deaths, increasing economic inequality, evictions, frontline employment. . . . And this seems to be a global story. COVID-19 is devasting to all regardless of age, geography, or social location. Each of us has experienced some disruptions in our life, whether we can no longer share a hug or find safe housing, or whether we have experienced the death of a loved one, we are all affected. Not necessarily equally, but we are all affected.

Regardless of geographic or social location, Black women find themselves occupying the forward-facing spaces of COVID-19. The story told here is limited as data were not always readily available, and such data are concentrated in certain countries. But this is what we know:

- There is a feminization of care work, and much of that care work is being carried out by poor women, immigrants, and women of color
- Stay-at-home orders exacerbate gender violence
- Black women have to provide care across multiple fronts, both in and outside of their homes
- Black women face economic, housing, and job insecurity
- Black women are stressed
- COVID-19 maps onto existing structures of oppression

Data alone will never fully capture the impact of COVID-19—the fears, the hopes, the loss, or the possibilities it presented. What data allow us to do is glimpse the devastation of the virus. And so, I offer a glimpse at how COVID-19 has affected Diasporic Black women. While the world may be opening back up, the pandemic is not over as we continue to see variants of the virus and hundreds of deaths across the globe. This limits the story that I offer below on the impact of COVID-19. Also limiting this story is the nature of data collection.

The challenge of analyzing the impact of COVID-19 on African/ African Diaspora/Black women, especially across geographic locations, is that data are not systematically collected. In the United States, Johns Hopkins University, early in the pandemic, established the Coronavirus Resources Center (https://coronavirus.jhu.edu). This digital platform offers a global map and a more specific U.S. map to track COVID-19 cases and deaths. As of January 2, 2021, there were 28,887 cases in South Africa, 6,348 in Guyana, and 395 in Barbados. The United States reported over 20 million cases and 342,300 deaths. The United Nations also offers comprehensive global data on COVID-19 cases and resulting deaths. The systemic problem is that the data do not provide within-group analysis, and data are not systematically collected to allow for comparisons. Thus, we know that in the United States, as of the writing of this chapter (March 2021), 1 in 562 Black Americans had died, proportionally more than for any other race (COVID Tracking Project 2021), and roughly 197,470 women had died (Centers for Diseases Control and Prevention, n.d.). We have no data on how many Black women have been infected and died because of the virus. And this is a challenge globally. For all the conversation on disparate impacts and the recognition that viruses affect communities along social location, in 2020, amid a pandemic, society is not collecting data that recognize that some of us are simultaneously Black and women, for example. One would have thought

that the HIV/AIDS pandemic would have informed how data are collected, and we would do differently as we face COVID-19.

Here is what we know. COVID-19, like HIV and AIDS, is being
mapped onto existing societal inequities. Consequently, COVID-19,
like HIV and AIDS, has a disparate impact on African/Black women,
and this is the case across geographic locations. And as with HIV
and AIDS, COVID's impact is both direct and indirect, and it is
financial and emotional, physical, and psychological. To begin to
craft a picture of how African/African Diaspora/Black women are
experiencing COVID-19, I offer data on some variables, treating
them in a discrete manner and recognizing that the impact is indeed
nonlinear. I present data on maternal and child health, followed by
the financial implications, African/African Diaspora/Black women's
mental health, housing insecurity, interpartner violence, and other
violences. To focus on the multiplicity of Blackness and gender, I
offer some data on COVID's impact on Black women with disabilities
and transgender women (no data were evident for African women
along with this metric). As a Black woman, I do this as we *need* to
have our story recorded in history so that we are not vanished in the
way that Black women were vanished in the recording of the Spanish
flu of 1918–19.

Maternal Health

What do we know from the past? According to Dorit Stein, Kevin
Ward, and Catherine Cantelmo (2020),

> During the Ebola epidemic in West Africa in 2014–2016, the use of
> reproductive and maternal healthcare services plummeted so much
> that maternal and neonatal deaths and stillbirths indirectly caused by
> the epidemic outnumbered direct Ebola-related deaths. . . . Some of
> these women stopped going to facilities due to fear of infection and in-
> creased physical and financial barriers. Others were denied care if they

were suspected of having Ebola as many facilities were not equipped to provide maternal healthcare to infected women.

COVID-19 is resulting in similar patterns, with women being particularly nervous and hesitant to seek medical care (Gordon 2021; Goyal et al., 2021). In Latin America and the Caribbean, women and children face extreme health conditions that may result in declines in any health progress they have made over the years. In other words, women and children face a regression in their health. As so, we can anticipate increases in maternal mortality, for example (UNICEF and the UN Development Programme 2020). Black women in the United Kingdom are five times as likely as their white counterparts to experience a pregnancy-related death (Reuters 2020). In the United States they are three to four times as likely to die (National Partnership for Women & Families 2018). In Brazil, Black-identified women also face pregnancy and postpartum challenges (Santos et al. 2021).

"COVID-19 exacerbates the issues around Black maternal health," says Marcela Howell, president of In Our Own Voice: National Black Women's Reproductive Justice Agenda (quoted in Supermajority Education Fund 2020). The challenges faced by pregnant women are multifaceted. For example, increased food insecurity can result in malnutrition and micronutrient deficiencies, which can cause harm to not only the woman but also the fetus. Consequently, both mother and child can face an increased risk of infection and death. Pregnant, low-income, and lower-resourced women also face the challenge of accessing quality care (a challenge that existed before COVID-19 and is now worsened). Women are experiencing limited availability of essential health-care services, and in some cases, women are giving birth without their partners or even a companion (see Bobrow 2020). COVID-19 has also affected reproductive care in general. As such, some women are experiencing limited access to abortion and birth control, resulting from both logistical challenges and ongoing political threats that limit access (Connor et al. 2020).

Financial Impact

Stagnant wages, underemployment, and poverty were all part of Black women's experiences before COVID-19. Black women have not all had the same economic experience resulting from the downturn in the economy. I hold myself as an example. My job has allowed me to shelter in place while working remotely. While it is important to recognize that Black women are not all the same and do not have the same experiences, I concentrate on those who have been disproportionately affected. I believe that we are only strong when all of us can freely pursue a safe and secure life.

Black women are disproportionately economically poor. Data tell us that Black workers (and also Indigenous and Hispanic workers), relative to white workers, face greater and increasing economic insecurity from COVID-19. According to Elise Gould and Valerie Wilson (2020), "There are three main groups of workers in the COVID-19 economy: those who have lost their jobs and face economic insecurity, those who are classified as essential workers and face health insecurity as a result, and those who are able to continue working from the safety of their homes." Overwhelmingly, Black women are not in the third category of workers. In the United States, Black women find themselves categorized as "essential" and "frontline" workers. This has translated into them and their families facing extreme risk. According to the National Women's Law Center, in the United States more than one in three Black-identified women serve as essential workers in frontline jobs. These women work as sales personnel, nursing assistants, health-care workers, and domestic care workers. It is also estimated that many of these women are immigrants (see Neely 2020). Given their place in the employment sector, many of these women have no safety net to buffer them from unemployment and have limited to no access to health care.

Mental Health

The overall well-being of Black women tends to be precarious even in "normal" times. Much of this precarity manifests in terms of "stress" and other mental health issues and is a result, in part, of the race-gender-class oppression many Black women face. This precarity persists during COVID-19. Consider that "Black pregnant women reported greater likelihood of having their employment negatively impacted, more concerns about a lasting economic burden, and more worries about their prenatal care, birth experience, and post-natal needs" (Gur et al. 2020). Black pregnant women are stressed. Jade Connor and colleagues (2020) tell us that "multifactorial stress is uniquely exacerbated among women during Covid-19." Additionally, Black communities tend to have lower access to mental health and substance abuse care. The stay-at-home orders have worsened this. Their frontline status, the need to "teach" and monitor school-age children from home, and financial and housing instability in conjunction with the continued assaults on Black bodies all contribute to the level of stress faced by Black women during COVID-19 (Anderson 2020).

Housing Insecurity

By all accounts, COVID has worsened housing insecurity for those already at the edge of finding and maintaining stable housing. According to the Center for American Progress,

> Before COVID-19, half of all renters were moderately or severely cost-burdened, with at least 30 to 50 percent of their household income going toward housing costs. Cost-burdened renters, particularly those of color, are the most at risk of eviction due to the increased likelihood of missing rent payments. People of color, who have faced higher rates of lost employment during the pandemic, continue to be disproportionately cost-burdened and at increased risk of eviction. (Lake 2020)

Before the pandemic, Black women were disproportionately exposed to evictions (Desmond 2014), and this has only worsened during the pandemic, given the economic insecurity they face.

In response to economic insecurity caused by the pandemic recession, the U.S. federal government issued an eviction moratorium as part of the CARES Act of March 2020. This moratorium prohibits landlords from filing new evictions in federally supported or financed housing. Initially, the moratorium was set to expire in July 2020, and it was extended through January 2021. While it prevented eviction, it did not recuse renters from paying rent. Thus, Black women who benefited from the mortarium still have to find a way to pay their rent or face eviction. What we know is that Black women are facing severe economic insecurity. A CNN headline from January 2021 read, "the US economy lost 140,000 jobs in December. All of them were held by women" (Kurtz 2021). That was just one headline. Another headline, in the *Cut* in November 2020, declared, "COVID Is Pushing Black Mothers Out of the Workforce at a Staggering Rate" (Aggeler 2020). In Canada, Black women are also experiencing the highest unemployment rates of any group (Gordon 2020). So, it is anticipated that they will face a similar situation as Black women in the United States. Many African nations are also facing increasing housing instability. According to a report issued by the UN-Habitat (2020, 10), "Risks of housing eviction due to lack of income and consequential rent arrears are thus high. In Africa, the share of people renting their accommodation can be as high as 70% in urban areas." Black women, regardless of geographic location, face a perilous situation regarding housing. Many of us cannot afford housing and are constantly facing being unhoused, and COVID has worsened this reality.

Interpartner Violence and Other Violences

Black women experience multiple forms of violence. The United Nations (n.d.) reports that prior to the pandemic, "243 million women and girls, aged 15–49 experienced sexual and/or physical violence by an intimate partner in the past year." The report says that since the onset of the pandemic, "domestic violence has intensified." While the factors that expose women to interpartner violence (IPV) are the same regardless of the pandemic, the pandemic has exacerbated women's exposure to violence.

Researchers have highlighted several factors that influence Black women's exposure to IPV. It is suggested that Black women's overexposure to structural violence, racism, sexism, and poverty, as well as their lack of access to health care, contributes to their disproportionate experience with IPV (Bent-Goodley 2001; Hampton, Oliver, and Magarian 2003). Beth E. Richie (1996, 2012), in addition to other researchers, centers identity, race, gender, and class, among other identity markers, as factors that influence how Black women experience IPV and how they are treated by law enforcement. Stereotypes, such as the emasculating Black woman, are also thought of as a factor shaping Black women's experiences with IPV (see Bell and Mattis 2000; Bent-Goodley 2005, 2007; Gillum 2009; West 2004).

In the United States, Black women accounted for 30 percent of all IPV-related deaths among all women in the years prior to COVID-19 (Petrosky et al. 2017). Nonwhite women in the United Kingdom also face a disproportionate impact with IPV (Femi-Ajao 2018). Women in Nigeria (Benebo, Schumann, and Vaezghasemi 2018) and Jamaica (Turner-Jones 2020) are also facing high rates of IPV.

Often framed as a pandemic within the pandemic, Black women's experiences with IPV seem to have been exacerbated during COVID-19. This situation has worsened because many women now find themselves sheltering in place with their abusers, with limited financial resources due to the economic downturn, and with limited access to public spaces or social networks. As Tamara Y. Jeffries (2020) writes, "It's a formula that puts sisters at an even greater risk of physical, emotional or financial abuse."

Black Women Living with Disabilities, Incarceration, and Transgenderism

There is much ado about Black women's exposure to COVID-19. Some of us are engaging in conversations that bring us to a postpandemic period and the question of how we begin to build infrastructure to support Black women. However, amid these conversations, some bodies are missing. Incarcerated and transgender Black women and those with disabilities are shadow bodies (see Jordan-Zachery 2017) in the public discourses on COVID-19. Their absence is in part due to how data are collected. Data are collected on race or gender while often ignoring that some are simultaneously raced and gendered. Part of the story of how some bodies go missing also has to do with boundaries (see Cohen 1999), and the decision about who is allowed into public discourse is the result of policing the boundaries of "normal" and respectable.

"Black people with disabilities are in a health equity crisis in the United States that is compounded by the COVID-19 pandemic—we just don't know exactly how bad it is" (Young 2020). Daniel Young is not exaggerating when he claims that we simply do not know how Black individuals with disabilities, and Black women specifically, are experiencing COVID-19. Black feminists speak of invisibility and the need to bring Black women from the margin to the center. If there was ever a need for us to systematically apply this, it is now. One in four Black-identified individuals are living with a disability (Courtney-Long et al. 2017). Research tells us that this population faces challenges in securing employment (Mitra and Kruse 2016), accessing health care (Campbell et al. 2009), and finding affordable housing. We can ill afford not to pay attention, socially and politically, to how Black women with disabilities are experiencing and living with COVID-19. Thus, we need to expand the boundaries to make space for the needs of Black women with disabilities.

And it is the same case for incarcerated Black girls and women. Black girls in the United States are more than three times as likely, in comparison to white girls, to be locked up. Black women are almost twice as likely to be incarcerated relative to their white counterparts (Sentencing Project 2020). In an interview with journalist Nick Charles (2020), Donna Hylton (a previously incarcerated prison activist) stated, "These populations are medically compromised long before incarceration. We didn't have resources before incarceration, imagine the communities inside prisons and jails." Incarcerated Black women experience limited testing and medical resources, and social distancing is unavailable. Consequently, "By May 14 [2020], Black inmates encompassed 60 percent of COVID-19 deaths in New York's prison system, even though they were around 50 percent of the state's incarcerated population" (ACLU 2020). We need to discuss how incarcerated Black girls and women are disappearing right before our eyes as they become ill or die in prisons and jails.

Also in the shadow of our public discourse are Black transgender women and the ways in which they are living with COVID-19. According to the 2015 U.S. Transgender Survey (James, Brown, and Wilson 2017), Black transgender people face the most severe economic and housing effects among lesbian, gay, bisexual, transgender, and queer (LGBTQ+) communities. The same survey tells the story of their overexposure to violence, homelessness, and poverty, as well as their limited access to shelters, health care, and the labor market. The Black LGBTQ+ population faces a number of structural risk factors as described above, and many people experience isolation from families, thus heightening their vulnerability to COVID-19. At the time of this writing, no data spoke to how many Black transgender individuals were affected by COVID-19, or how. Consequently, the story of this group is relatively sparse, not because we do not want to tell the story but because the data are so limited.

As societies attempt to manage COVID-19 and imagine a life post COVID, we need to hear about African/African Diaspora/Black women. We need to mark their experiences to know that they are here. One day, like the Spanish flu, COVID-19 will end. And Black women will be left wondering "when will the COVID be over?" as its impact will be long felt among us.

"I Am Here. Are You?" A Technique for "Finding" Black Women

"It is not enough to just collect narrative data," Janette Y. Taylor (1998, 59) tells us. Instead, "we must attempt to locate ourselves and perform research in ways that affirm African American women." And this is where testimony becomes useful as a method for unearthing African/African Diaspora/Black women's experiences with COVID-19: "Gaining insight into the everyday lives of African-American women and how they interpret them requires conscious methodological approaches and research practices" (Mullings 2000, 20). Testimony serves as a means for locating oneself and affirming African and African Diasporic women, thereby allowing us to get to the context-specific knowledge held by African/African Diaspora/Black women (also thought of as their standpoint). Through testimony, African/African Diaspora/Black women become "informants [who] are no longer simply talked to, but talk for themselves" (Few, Stephens, and Rouse-Arnett 2003, 207). A tradition of Black feminism is that Black women should be allowed to speak not just about their experiences but also from their own experiences (Hill Collins 2000). For us to better understand how African/African Diaspora/Black women are experiencing COVID-19, the women must tell their stories. This is why, in part, I organized *Lavender Fields: Black Women Experiencing Fear, Agency, and Hope in the Time of COVID-19*.

Lavender Fields is a bit of an ode to Alice Walker. Notably, it pays homage to Walker's telling of her story, her testimony, of how she worked to excavate Zora Neale Hurston's burial site. As part of her tale of searching for Zora, Walker (1975, 85) writes,

"How're you to find anything out here?" [a companion] asks. And I stand still a few seconds, looking at the weeds. Some of them are quite pretty, with tiny yellow flowers. They are thick and healthy but dead weeds under them have formed a thick gray carpet on the ground. . . . We move slowly, very slowly, our eyes alert, our legs trembly. . . . I take my bearings . . . and try to navigate to exact center. But the center of anything can be very large . . . finding the grave seems positively hopeless. There is only one thing to do:

"Zora!" I yell as loud as I can . . .

"Zora!" I call again. "I'm here. Are you?"

"I'm here. Are you?" I can imagine how Walker must have felt standing there searching for Zora Neale Hurston's unmarked and uncared-for grave. I imagine it the same way my mother's little neighbor stood on one side of the gate as her friend, my mother, stood on the other side. Each so close and yet so far. Each searching, pondering what was to come. Each in her way saying, "I'm here. Are you?"

Amid COVID-19, state-sanctioned violence, and economic downturn, Black women, regardless of location, are crying out, "I'm here. Are you?" As they work on the front lines as essential workers, as they shelter in place, as they get behind the mask, as they . . . who sees African/African Diaspora/Black women? And more importantly, how are they seen? Alice Walker worked diligently to find Zora. To ensure that we could find Zora. This book, *Lavender Fields*, attempts to "find" African/African Diaspora/Black women amid all that we are experiencing. And it is not so much that we are lost, but more that we are often not seen. Our fields, while blooming in some areas, are left unattended in others.

Black women have a way of knowing. I use Alice Walker's way of knowing, as detailed in her quest to locate Zora's resting place, to offer a technique for engaging Black women's testimonies of their experiences with COVID-19. I use the term *technique* intentionally as terms such as *methods* and *methodology* can take us into a place of Western philosophic understanding and, as such, can decenter Black women's ways of knowing (see Hill Collins 2000). Using Alice Walker's account of her journey to find Zora Neale Hurston's grave, I craft a four-pronged technique that centers Black women's way of knowing as a means of engaging their testimonies as captured across the ten essays and thought pieces. The four elements—markers, the in-between space of knowing–unknowing–not knowing, community and lineage, and desires—speak to the radical curation that Black girls and women engage in when they declare "I am here!"

Element 1: Markers

It was not enough for Walker to simply locate Zora's grave; she had to erect a marker. The grave marker reads, "ZORA NEALE HURSTON / 'A GENIUS OF THE SOUTH' / 1901–1960 / NOVELIST, FOLKLORIST / ANTHROPOLOGIST," thereby inviting us not only to see Zora but to understand her and the work she did. All her books were out of print at the time of Walker's sojourn to find Zora. Zora Neale Hurston had faded into obscurity. Some folks from her hometown did not know of her or had never read her works (Walker 1975). Thus, this marker allowed Walker to resurrect the dead through the process of naming and defining—which then allowed the unknown to become known.

As a form of speech/narrative, markers are meant to offer both context and voice. As such, they provide psychic space for reclamation, recovery, and healing. Markers declare "I am here," and consequently, we (Black women) are here. A marker allows the unseen to be seen. In the case of Zora, the physical grave marker is a form of radical curation. And markers allow us to speak beyond ourselves, thus bending time. Through markers, we can go into the past, stay in the present, and speak to the future. They do not just respond "we are here"; they show how and when we are here, in space and through time. In writing about Black girls' curation, Ashleigh Greene Wade

(2018, 21) says that "archiving [is] not necessarily in terms of preserving or documenting 'true' events or a 'true' self but rather as a method of space-making, a process of transforming garrets ([to reference the theory of Katherine] McKittrick), which constitutes a particularly important one for Black girls who constantly receive messages admonishing them to take up as little space as possible." Markers challenge invisibility, hence offering a context that becomes a reference point or a framework that situates the individual or group in action, time, and space. In this case, they allow Black women to take up space—physical and psychic space.

Furthermore, markers allow for disruption of existing narratives not only by bearing witness to an existence but also by affirming power—the power to define oneself. Markers indicate ownership of space; as such, a marker in and of itself becomes a knowledge holder that allows for particular definitions and understandings. Finally, markers make public, enhancing the accessibility of memory and, by extension, knowledge. Consequently, markers are a way of combatting forgetting and erasure.

Throughout *Lavender Fields*, we are presented with several markers that are designed to counter namelessness and invisibility and that move us, Black women, from object to subject. These markers are part of Black girls' and women's curation of self. The authors show us how they tap into the spiritual realm, the ancestorial realm, and how they imagine the future in the present to craft themselves through and beyond COVID-19. reelaviolette botts-ward illustrates how she literally curated herself, creating markers of her experience via visual art. Brianna Y. Clark relies on actual grave markers to explore how the knowledge of her ancestors allowed her to access different narratives of Black female survival—narratives that helped her negotiate and navigate COVID-19. Nimot Ogunfemi captures the functioning of markers when she writes, "A Black transnational feminist positionality allowed me to embrace and critique the global moment, encouraged me to wander freely in transformative spiritual spaces, and facilitated the study of my soul." Kyrah K. Brown and colleagues remind us that there is a need to center Black women's voices in health research, practice, and policymaking. And Annet Matebwe explores what happens when policymaking fails to account for African immigrant women in the context of the United Kingdom. What she does in this reflective essay is detail how the absence of markers leads to invisibility and why Black women must speak—radically curating themselves. She writes,

> I was invisible but yet felt targeted in a particular way. . . . Although one might argue that being unemployed during the pandemic wasn't a unique position as thousands of other people were in the same predicament, I'd beg to differ. Here's why: many immigrant workers are concentrated within the hospitality and beauty industries, the industries that the government deemed nonessential during the lockdown. This meant that although the national lockdown was meant to affect people equally, immigrant workers, like myself, were, in fact, the hardest hit by the government's decision to shut down the hospitality and beauty industries. . . . Sharing my thoughts and experiences of living as a Black immigrant woman in the United Kingdom is not earth-shattering information. But I believe it is a story worth sharing because it highlights some of the ignored problems brought about when governments make decisions that do not account for the individuals such as me, those who are simultaneously Black, woman, and immigrant.

Radscheda Nobles offers the marker of the experiences of a differently abled Black woman. She tells us that she writes as it provides her with a "place in academia to tell my experience and advocate for myself as a differently abled Black woman in a space where my voice is often ignored."

Across the ten essays and thought pieces we see how Black women curate themselves, and how, like Walker, they do not simply share the result of the process—the actual curation—but take us on the journey of creating markers. This is seen in their use of autoethnography. According to Layla D. Brown-Vincent (2019, 124), "The most critical contribution of Black Feminist Autoethnography is that of presenting oppositional knowledge which demonstrates the ways in which our individual preoccupations are linked by histories of struggle, as well as our liberation. Furthermore, the work of Black Feminist Autoethnographers is to document that which we always, already know to be true, that our fates are linked, and the struggle continues." Using autoethnography, the authors are not simply explaining or describing their experiences with COVID-19; they are engaging in a critique of larger structures that tend to disappear Black women, like Zora was disappeared, like the Black women who endured the Spanish flu were disappeared. Through their theorizing and operationalizing of their experiences, they have answered the call *I am here*, which furthers African/African Diaspora/Black girls' and women's ongoing quest for liberation. Through their autoethnography, we see how Black girls and women are disrupting race-gender-ability/disability narratives and systems of inequality. In other words, they are using their experiences as markers to right the world.

Element 2: The In-Between Space of Knowing–Unknowing–Not Knowing

Alice Walker engages Homi Bhabha's concept of the Third Space in her search for Zora Neale Hurston. In speaking on the Third Space, Bhabha (2004, 56) says,

> The theoretical recognition of the split-space of enunciation may open the way to conceptualizing an international culture based . . . on the inscription and articulation of culture's hybridity. . . . It is the "inter"— the cutting edge of translation and negotiation, the in-between space— that carries the burden and meaning of culture. It makes it possible to begin envisaging national, antinationalist histories of the "people." And

by exploring this Third Space, we may elude the politics of polarity and emerge as the others of our selves.

Although Bhabha's concept of Third Space is about colonization, I find it beneficial in this context as it speaks to the creation of frontiers (other ways of being) that sit "in-between," where one can come to know self, individually and collectively, where identities are reshaped or even invented. And it is in this Third Space that one can experience freedom. I think of this space as one of knowing–unknowing–not knowing.

In her telling of her journey to find Zora, Walker walks us through this process of sitting "in-between." For example, we see how she unknows her knowledge of the cause of Zora's death or even what she looked like. Walker (1975, 87) writes of a conversation she had with someone who was familiar with Zora: "'I was surprised to learn she died of malnutrition.'... 'Zora *didn't* die of malnutrition,' [Dr. Benton] says indignantly.... 'She had a stroke, and she died in the welfare home.'" Further into her conversation with Dr. Benton, Walker unlearns her image of Zora, and she learns, "she was a big woman, *erect*.... And she weighed about two hundred pounds. Probably more. She ..." Walker cuts him off: "What! Zora was *fat!*" (emphasis in original).

There were some things that Walker knew about Zora, some things she had to learn, and other things she had to unlearn. But what does this have to do with African/African Diaspora/Black girls' and women's experiences with COVID-19?

COVID-19 caused all of us—at least I would like to hope all of us—to think about what we know, what we do not know, and what we needed to unknow. COVID-19 allowed many of us to sit in that in-between space where we could come to see ourselves. Sara Jean-Francois shows us her process of knowing, not knowing, and unknowing, and she reveals how, when she sat in that in-between space, she was better able to understand the knowledge held in the Haitian community around healing. Jean-Francois relied on the ancestral healing knowledge used by her mother, who nursed her back to health after she was stricken by COVID-19. She writes that she knew of how Black women were ignored by some in the medical profession, how she had to unknow that she may have been treated differently, and ultimately how she had to come to know the power of ancestral healing. Jean-Francois states, "For many, ancestral healing knowledge, or traditional cultural remedies, may seem nonscientific, or perhaps too obvious. Still, my culture and mother have taught me that our bodies are a healing force, and a powerful one at that. This pandemic has only brought to light how powerful generational knowledge, cultural remedies, and a mother's healing can really be."

Angela K. Lewis-Maddox shows us, rather poignantly, what it means to find self in a space of despondency and what it took to fight for herself—her sense of recovering from this feeling. Her feelings of despondence resulted from the intersection of COVID-19 and race-gender inequitable treatment she experienced at her job. She writes, "I entered the pandemic broken, hurt, and despondent." She knew that she needed to "get it together." However, "the idea of simply getting it together is troubling, considering the systems of oppression under which the Black community, particularly Black women, exist." What this required is that Lewis-Maddox had to learn other ways of being. She had to curate herself by learning to breathe. And Kyrah K. Brown and colleagues speak of a "looking glass" through which faith—Islamic faith, for example—allowed rest in that in-between space of coming to know self. It is not that these women were simply engaged in the act of knowing–unknowing–not knowing for individualistic purposes. They entered this in-between space to engage in self-curation to come into a world in a way that allowed for resistance to oppression and the crafting of a different here and now and future.

The knowledge that comes from sitting in that space of knowing–unknowing–not knowing consists, to borrow from Vrinda Dalmiya and Linda Alcoff (1993), of "knowing how" and "knowing what it is like" rather than the traditional "knowing that." This is because knowledge is not simply "found in words but in habits of being and the way one lives" (hooks 1996, 52). What happens when we sit in that in-between space? When we give ourselves permission to sit in this space, we can feel, see, and hear. As the essays and thought pieces in this collection show us, sitting in this space allows for a discovery of truth, not some universal truth and not a truth that rests in individualism. Instead, it is a truth that embodies the experiences we rely on, that which is intimately familiar, the experiences of the individual who understands themselves as part of a larger group, thereby challenging the notion of the separation of the *I* and *we*. This is a process that can bring us closer to freedom.

Sitting in that in-between space of knowing–unknowing–not knowing offers a new/different set of analytic categories by exposing constraints, thereby giving way to a type of attention that allows for the imagination of other forms of being. In thinking of "spaces of possibility," Jessica Robertson (2019, 5) writes that such spaces allow us to "uncover new meanings in the past, ease constraints of vision in the 'now,' and allow recognition of the previous life of narratives in the present." This is precisely what it means to dwell in the in-between space of knowing–unknowing–not knowing. More specifically, this space allows for the bending of time. And we see how Alice Walker bends time in her search for Zora by dwelling in this space. She had to (re)learn the cause of Zora's death, manage Zora's disappearance from the literary world, and introduce Zora to a newer generation of individuals who lived in the home across from hers. And the essays and thought pieces that make up *Lavender Fields* do the same.

Element 3: Community and Lineage
Dwelling in this space of the knowing–unknowing–not knowing allowed Alice Walker also to find her voice, a voice that was part of the lineage of Zora Neale Hurston. In the tale of finding Zora, Walker

draws attention to the sites of loss (and what we do not know because
of these sites of loss) and memory (what we do know), brings them
into the present while making a way for a future (what we know and
do not know), and does so by being in community. As Patricia Hill
Collins (2016) argues, the notion of "self" is not defined as the increased autonomy gained by separation from others. The self exists
in relation. Consequently, the connectedness between the self and
others can give way to a deeper and more meaningful form of self-
definition/articulation, empowerment, and group solidarity. And we
see this in Walker's search for Zora, which resulted from Walker's
belief that they were connected. In her *In Search of Our Mothers' Gardens* (1983), Walker positions herself in the lineage of great African
American female writers and as the metaphorical daughter of Hurston. Through placing herself in this lineage, Walker (1975, 85, 87) un-
dertakes a "fight for Zora and her work" because this work "must not
be lost to us" and the fight is part of her "duty." Additionally, Walker
(1983, 12) argues that Hurston is a "model" for herself: "What I had
discovered, of course, was a model. A model, who, as it happened,
provided more than voodoo for my story, more than one of the great-
est novels America had produced—though, being America, it did not
realize this. She had provided, as if she knew someday I would come
along wandering in the wilderness, a nearly complete record of her
life. And though her life sprouted an occasional wart, I am eternally
grateful for that life, warts and all." As part of her politics to subvert
a racist-sexist literary canon that disappeared Black women writers,
Walker uses Zora Neale Hurston as a model to move beyond racism
and sexism—thus making a way for equity and justice.

   Lavender Fields embodies Walker's understandings of community
and lineage. The authors show us how they rely on community when
time slows down, our fears increase, and we need time to imagine our
hopes and dreams. Mbali Mazibuko asks, "When grief sits on our chest,
as an almost perpetual condition of being a Black woman, is there

room for us to move alongside it in modes of joy and community?" She then shows how Black South African women use the Xhosa phrases *semhle* and *sbwl* ("You are beautiful" and "craving," respectively) to be in community—by cooking and using fashion in online spaces to come together as a means of managing COVID-19. As she argues, "the longing to be in the presence of loved ones, to sbwl, was alternated with our sharing of food and recipes online, where we turn a supposedly oppressive thing into a pleasurable and community-building exercise." Elizabeth Peart speaks to how community helped her overcome her fears of contracting COVID-19. She describes how her school friends helped her work through her fears—naming them and finding a way to overcome them. Angela K. Lewis-Maddox explores the value of "sacred" community organized through an online writing group and how that allowed her to heal and feel empowered. reelaviolette bottsward says, "From sonic healing arts to downtown murals of mourning, Black womxn artists saved me from losing my mind this year." Nimot Ogunfemi relies on the community of such groups as the Women of Irmandande da Boa Morte, and the political and spiritual healing work of such women to inform her own "ritual of research."

This brings me to experiential knowledge and how it allows us to explore the functioning of community. Using experiential knowledge, in the way that Walker used such knowledge in her search for Zora, the authors sense gaps/fissures vis-à-vis their experiences. And they also feel possibilities for growth and expression. Kyrah K. Brown and colleagues offer an example of this functioning of community. For one, there are nine authors on this piece, and in speaking with them as they wrote this chapter, I could see how they were dependent on community as a space of healing and managing the fears of COVID-19. Using their individual and collective experiences, the authors demonstrate how the limiting notion of the "Superwoman schema" had to be challenged for them to engage in a practice of "liberation and resistance." They tell of their struggles with gaps that are grounded in controlling images of Black women, in their larger efforts to promote health equity.

Additionally, some authors use their experiences to show how community often leaves some behind. Radscheda Nobles explains how differently abled Black women are often not seen and thus not cared for in community. She shows the value of including a population perpetually at the margins within intersectional theory—Black women living with disabilities—in policymaking. Elizabeth Peart maps her experience with COVID-19 onto racial inequality to expose gaps in society by looking at how both racism and COVID-19 heightened her feelings of difference and the notion of the "other," thereby exposing power structures and social constructions that rest in illness and also in race-gender. Using her positionality as a Zimbabwean immigrant living in the United Kingdom, Annet Matebwe shows fissures in her community by exposing how government policies left her vulnerable to economic uncertainty.

In telling of her search for Zora, Walker taps into the value of community—a Black women's community—and lineage. A communal approach grounded in lineage is valuable as it allows us to see and enable the Black female possibility of self and others. The telling of testimonies vis-à-vis autoethnography encourages sharing and retelling of lived experiences. (Re)telling these stories can bring members of a community together through shared knowledge and experiences while exposing gaps and possibilities for a different future for community members. Using lineage and community allows for self-actualization/realization.

Community engagement involves listening and suggests that data gathering is interactional. But, some may wonder, is this only available to interviews? How can it be used with text? This project is an example of how this work is done with text. Consider that the work was birthed by listening to the ancestors—allowing them to speak. I simply listened. They had their call; *Julia, are you here?*

Furthermore, the organization of this book is influenced by the work of Gloria Anzaldúa, Leith Mullings, Zora Neale Hurston, and other women whose voices are not recorded in text—lineage. These women placed themselves in community and grounded their work in experiential knowledge as a means of ensuring that those of us on the margin are not disappeared. They are forever answering the call "Are you here?" According to Walker (1983, 373), "We are together, my child and I. Mother and child, yes, but sisters really, against whatever denies us all that we are." The ideography of community and lineage decenters neocapitalism's notion of individualism, allowing for group solidarity.

Element 4: Desires

Johnnetta B. Cole argues that a Black feminist anthropologist's work must *do* something; it must "participate in some way in the active struggle against racism, sexism, and all other systems of inequality" (Heyward-Rotimi 1998, 4). Black women's expression of their desires is this doing of something. There is a practice and politics involved in Black women's stating their desires. Its politics is that it talks back to a practice of invisibility and resulting inequities. Black women's declaration of their desires speaks to their hopes and dreams of survival, and to their imagination of a future while making it real in the present, a world where their existence is neither challenged nor erased. In *Black Feminist Criticism*, Barbara Christian (1986, 159) points out that "a persistent and major theme throughout Afro-America women's literature [is] our attempt to define and express our totality rather than being defined by others."

Walker (1975, 76) captures the politics of Black women's desires to define themselves when she recounts her interaction with Mrs. Moseley as she searched for Zora Neale Hurston. In response to a question about her thoughts on integration, Mrs. Moseley answers: "I have the blood of three races in my veins . . . white, black and Indian, and nobody asked me *anything* before" (emphasis in original). Mrs. Moseley identifies herself as a colored woman. She suggests that her identity is a wellspring of knowledge, yet it is overlooked. Black feminist scholars write extensively about how Black women's knowledge is often ignored (Hill Collins 2016). And they suggest that Black women, given their standpoint, offer a critique of oppressive structures while advocating for a more democratic society. A classic example of such is the "Black Feminist Statement" from the Combahee River Collective (2014). Like Ms. Moseley's declaration, the Combahee River Collective statement is one of desire—Black women's political practice to assert themselves so that they may be free.

This political practice is captured across the essays and thought pieces of *Lavender Fields*. In the poem that introduces the volume, LeConté J. Dill tells us of her desire for a knotless back that would remind her "not to hold / my breath [nor] grind my teeth." This knotless back can be read as a desire for freedom and autonomy. reelaviolette botts-ward demonstrates how she grapples with "broader themes of safety, protection, refusal, and remorse" to engage in "Black Feminist Interior Design." The notion of a Black feminist interior design, not named as such, is also a thread in Elizabeth Peart's "Reflections on COVID from a Ten-Year-Old Black Queen," where she shows how she maps her experiences with COVID-19 and anti-Black violence. She exposes her interior fears of not being accepted as a way of showing how these experiences collide in her life and, ultimately, undergird her desire to be free. Kyrah K. Brown and colleagues, in articulating their desires, state, "The authors describe their liberation and resistance, which involves an intentional effort to recenter and redefine their roles with an eye to what success in their roles can and will look like." They articulate a desire for self-articulation. As we manage what Brianna Y. Clark refers to as an "existential crisis," she reminds us, similarly to Sara Jean-Francois, that we can rest in the knowledge of our ancestors and lineage; they show us a desire to connect across generations, as part of our goal to make ourselves and our communities whole. And this was, in part, the impetus for Walker's desire to find Zora—to help us be whole.

Nimot Ogunfemi informs us that we need not be afraid to enter the "dark space" to find and state our desires. As she argues, "For me, the dark has proven to be a space of spiritual reconnection and true authenticity. It is the space that allows for the most accurate self/soul reflection." Entering that dark place, the place that affords us the opportunity for "Black Feminist Interior Design," not only unknots our backs by allowing us to examine and manage our "economies of grief" (as Mbali Mazibuko writes) but affords us the possibility of engaging in "pleasurable and community-building exercise" such as that described by Mazibuko.

Conclusion

bell hooks (1991, 8) asserts, "personal testimony, personal experience, is such fertile ground for the production of liberatory feminist theory because usually, it forms the base of our theory-making." By offering the personal testimonies and experiences of Black girls and women affected by COVID-19, *Lavender Fields* provides us an opportunity to build theory. A theory that will bring us closer to freedom. The authors of *Lavender Fields*, through the sharing of their testimonies, show us how they have engaged in radical curation, vis-à-vis creating markers, going into in-between spaces of knowing–unknowing–not knowing to enhance memories, and stating their desires as part of the I/we to ensure that their experiences are not forgotten. The four-pronged technique I describe above, originating in Alice Walker's desire to find Zora Neale Hurston, affords us a means for understanding, deeper, how African/African Diaspora/Black women engage in radical curation. Combined, the four-pronged technique shows us how to combat the forgetting and erasure that tend to follow African/

African Diaspora/Black women, thereby allowing for a definition of life based on lived experiences. By accessing memory and, by extension, knowledge, African/African Diaspora/Black women are offered political and cultural spaces for alliances and community building. But more importantly, the four-pronged technique in the words of the girls and women who worked in community to make *Lavender Fields* real shows us how to

Enter a *Black Feminist Interior Space*,
where we are never alone in spirit.
By engaging in the *timeless call-and-response* of our ancestors
and their *ancestral healing knowledge*,
which allows us to recognize and manage the *daily struggle* of
COVID-19 and other oppressive structures.
Unknotting our backs,
so that we can make *space where (our) voice* is not ignored
as our *story is worth sharing* because it highlights ignored problems.
And in telling these stories, we are able to *just BREATHE*,
resting in *my* (our) *power, my* (our) *peace, my* (our) *harmony*.
Not resting until justice is on (our) *side*.
World-making,
so that we can recognize one another and call out *Semhle, Sbwl*.
Then we will know that I/we are here.

References

ACLU West Virginia. 2020. "Racial Disparities in Jails and Prisons: COVID-19's Impact on the Black Community." June 12, 2020. https://www.acluwv.org/en/news/racial-disparities-jails-and-prisons-covid-19s-impact-black-community.

Aggeler, Madeline. 2020. "COVID Is Pushing Black Mothers Out of the Workforce at a Staggering Rate." *Cut*, November 12, 2020. https://www.thecut.com/2020/11/black-mothers-pushed-out-of-workforce-at-staggering-rate-covid.html.

Allen, Brenda J. 2009. "Black Feminist Epistemology." In *Encyclopedia of Communication Theory*, edited by Stephen W. Littlejohn and Karen A. Foss, 188–215. Thousand Oaks, Calif.: Sage.

Anderson, Riana. 2020. "Surviving the Coronavirus While Black: Pandemic's Heavy Toll on African American Mental Health." University of Michigan School of Public Health. May 20, 2020. https://sph.umich.edu/news/2020 posts/pandemics-toll-on-african-american-mental-health.html.

Bell, Carl C., and Jacqueline Mattis. 2000. "The Importance of Cultural Competence in Ministering to African American Victims of Domestic Violence." *Violence Against Women* 6 (5): 515–32.

Benebo, Faith Owunari, Barbara Schumann, and Masoud Vaezghasemi. 2018. "Intimate Partner Violence Against Women in Nigeria: A Multilevel Study Investigating the Effect of Women's Status and Community Norms." *BMC Women's Health* 18: article 136. https://doi.org/10.1186/s12905-018-0628-7.

Bent-Goodley, Tricia. 2001. "Eradicating Domestic Violence in the African American Community: A Literature Review and Action Agenda." *Trauma, Violence, & Abuse* 2 (4): 316–30.

Bent-Goodley, Tricia B. 2005. "Culture and Domestic Violence: Transforming Knowledge Development." *Journal of Interpersonal Violence* 20 (2): 195–203.

Bent-Goodley, Tricia B. 2007. "Health Disparities and Violence Against Women: Why and How Cultural and Societal Influences Matter." *Trauma, Violence, and Abuse* 8 (2): 90–104.

Bhabha, Homi. 2004. *The Location of Culture*. London: Routledge.

Bobrow, Emily. 2020. "A Chaotic Week for Pregnant Women in New York City." *New Yorker*, April 1, 2020. https://www.newyorker.com/science/medical-dispatch/a-chaotic-week-for-pregnant-women-in-new-york-city.

Boylorn, Robin. 2016. "On Being at Home with Myself: Blackgirl Autoethnography as Research Practice." *International Review of Qualitative Research* 9 (1): 44–58.

Brown-Vincent, Layla D. 2019. "Seeing It for Wearing It: Autoethnography as Black Feminist Methodology." *Taboo: The Journal of Culture and Education* 18 (1): 109–25.

Campbell, Vincent A., Jamylle A. Gilyard, Lisa Sinclair, Tom Sternberg, and June I. Kailes. 2009. "Preparing for and Responding to Pandemic Influenza: Implications for People with Disabilities." *American Journal of Public Health* 99 (S2): S294–S300.

Charles, Nick. 2020. "Black Female Inmates and COVID-19: Medically Compromised, Vulnerable and Neglected." *NBC News*, April 11, 2020. https://

www.nbcnews.com/news/nbcblk/black-female-inmates-covid-19-medically -compromised-vulnerable-neglected-n1189086.

Christian, Barbara. 1986. *Black Feminist Criticism: Perspectives on Black Women Writers*. New York: Teachers College Press.

Cohen, Cathy. 1999. *The Boundaries of Blackness: AIDS and the Breakdown of Black Politics*. Chicago: University of Chicago Press.

Combahee River Collective. 2014. "A Black Feminist Statement." *Women's Studies Quarterly* 42 (3–4): 271–80.

Connor, Jade, Sarina Madhavan, Mugdha Mokashi, Hanna Amanuel, Natasha R. Johnson, Lydia E. Pace, and Deborah Bartz. 2020. "Health Risks and Outcomes That Disproportionately Affect Women During the Covid-19 Pandemic: A Review." *Social Science and Medicine* 266: article 113364. https:// doi.org/10.1016/j.socscimed.2020.113364.

Courtney-Long, Elizabeth A., Sebastian D. Romano, Dianna D. Carroll, and Michael H. Fox. 2017. "Socioeconomic Factors at the Intersection of Race and Ethnicity Influencing Health Risks for People with Disabilities." *Journal of Racial and Ethnic Health Disparities* 4 (2): 213–22.

COVID Tracking Project. 2021. "The COVID Racial Data Tracker." Last updated March 7, 2021. https://covidtracking.com/race.

Dalmiya, Vrinda, and Linda Alcoff. 1993. "Are 'Old Wives' Tales' Justified?" In *Feminist Epistemologies*, edited by Linda Alcoff and Elizabeth Potter, 217– 44. New York: Routledge.

Desmond, Matthew. 2014. "Poor Black Women Are Evicted at Alarming Rates, Setting Off a Chain of Hardship." MacArthur Foundation: How Housing Matters. March 2014. https://www.macfound.org/media/files/HHM_Research _Brief_-_Poor_Black_Women_Are_Evicted_at_Alarming_Rates.pdf.

Dickens, Danielle D., Veronica Y. Womack, and Treshae Dimes. 2019. "Managing Hypervisibility: An Exploration of Theory and Research on Identity Shifting Strategies in the Workplace Among Black Women." *Journal of Vocational Behavior* 113: 153–63.

Durham, Aisha. 2017. "On Collards." *International Review of Qualitative Research* 10 (1): 22–23.

Femi-Ajao, Omolade. 2018. "Intimate Partner Violence and Abuse Against Nigerian Women Resident in England, UK: A Cross-Sectional Qualitative Study." *BMC Women's Health* 18: article 123. https://doi.org/10.1186/s12905 -018-0610-4.

Few, April L., Dionne P. Stephens, and Marlo Rouse-Arnett. 2003. "Sister-to-Sister Talk: Transcending Boundaries and Challenges in Qualitative Research with Black Women." *Family Relations: An Interdisciplinary Journal of Applied Family Studies* 52 (3): 205–15.

Gillum, Tameka L. 2009. "Improving Services to African American Survivors of IPV: From the Voices of Recipients of Culturally Specific Services." *Violence Against Women* 15 (1): 57–80.

Gordon, Deb. 2021. "Women Not Getting the Healthcare They Need During Covid-19, New Survey Shows." *Forbes*, March 26, 2021. https://www.forbes .com/sites/debgordon/2021/03/26/women-not-getting-the-healthcare-they -need-during-covid-19-new-survey-shows/.

Gordon, Julie. 2020. "Black, Minority Women in Canada Left Behind in COVID-19 Job Recovery." Reuters, December 15, 2020. https://www.reuters.com/article /us-health-coronavirus-canada-employment/black-minority-women-in -canada-left-behind-in-covid-19-job-recovery-idUSKBN28P2O2.

Gould, Elise, and Valerie Wilson. 2020. "Black Workers Face Two of the Most Lethal Preexisting Conditions for Coronavirus—Racism and Economic Inequality." Economic Policy Institute. June 1, 2020. https://www.epi.org/publi cation/black-workers-covid/.

Goyal, Manu, Pratibha Singh, Kuldeep Singh, Shashank Shekhar, Neha Agrawal, and Sanjeev Misra. 2021. "The Effect of the COVID-19 Pandemic on Maternal Health Due to Delay in Seeking Health Care: Experience from a Tertiary Center." *International Journal of Gynecology and Obstetrics* 152 (2): 231–35.

Gur, Raquel E., Lauren K. White, Rebecca Waller, Ran Barzilay, Tyler M. Moore, Sara Kornfield, Wanjiku F. M. Njoroge et al. 2020. "The Disproportionate Burden of the COVID-19 Pandemic Among Pregnant Black Women." *Psychiatry Research* 293: article 113475. https://doi.org/10.1016/j.psychres.2020.113475.

Hampton, Robert, William Oliver, and Lucia Magarian. 2003. "Domestic Violence in the African American Community: An Analysis of Social and Structural Factors." *Violence and Victims* 9 (5): 522–57.

Heyward-Rotimi, Kamela. 1998. "Perspectives of Black Feminist Anthropology: An Interview with Dr. Johnnetta B. Cole." *Voices* 2 (2): 1–5.

Hill Collins, Patricia. 2000. *Black Feminist Thought: Knowledge, Consciousness, and the Politics of Empowerment*. New York: Routledge.

Hill Collins, Patricia. 2016. "Black Feminist Thought as Oppositional Knowledge." *Departures in Critical Qualitative Research* 5 (3): 133–44.

hooks, bell. 1984. *Feminist Theory: From Margin to Center*. Cambridge: South End Press.

hooks, bell. 1989 *Talking Back: Thinking Feminist, Thinking Black*. Boston: South End Press.

hooks, bell. 1991. "Theory as Liberatory Practice." *Yale Journal of Law and Feminism* 4 (1): 1–12. https://digitalcommons.law.yale.edu/yjlf/vol4/iss1/2.

hooks, bell. 1996. "Choosing the Margin as a Space of Radical Openness." in *Women, Knowledge, and Reality*, edited by Ann Garry and Marilyn Pearsall, 48–55. London: Routledge.

James, Sandy E., Carter Brown, and Isaiah Wilson. 2017. *2015 U.S. Transgender Survey: Report on the Experiences of Black Respondents*. Washington, D.C.: National Center for Transgender Equality, Black Trans Advocacy, and National Black Justice Coalition. https://www.ustranssurvey.org/reports.

Jeffries, Tamara Y. 2020. "For Black Women Suffering Domestic Abuse, Coronavirus Quarantines Are Life Threatening." *Essence*, updated December 6, 2020. https://www.essence.com/news/domestic-violence-coronavirus/.

Jordan-Zachery, Julia S. 2017. *Shadow Bodies: Black Women, Ideology, Representation, and Politics*. New Brunswick, N.J.: Rutgers University.

Jordan-Zachery, Julia S., and Duchess Harris, eds. 2019. *Black Girl Magic Beyond the Hashtag: Twenty-First-Century Acts of Self-Definition*. Tucson: University of Arizona Press.

Kurtz, Annalyn. 2021. "The US Economy Lost 140,000 Jobs in December. All of Them Were Held by Women." *CNN Business*, January 8, 2021. https://www.cnn.com/2021/01/08/economy/women-job-losses-pandemic/index.html.

Lake, Jaboa. 2020. "The Pandemic Has Exacerbated Housing Instability for Renters of Color." Center for American Progress. October 30, 2020. https://www.americanprogress.org/issues/poverty/reports/2020/10/30/492606/pandemic-exacerbated-housing-instability-renters-color/.

Mitra, Sophie, and Douglas Kruse. 2016. "Are Workers with Disabilities More Likely to Be Displaced?" *International Journal of Human Resource Management* 27 (14): 1550–79.

Mullings, Leith. 2000. "African-American Women Making Themselves: Notes on the Role of Black Feminist Research." *Souls: A Critical Journal of Black Politics, Culture, and Society* 2 (4): 18–29.

National Partnership for Women & Families. 2018. *Black Women's Maternal Health: A Multifaceted Approach to Addressing Persistent and Dire Health Disparities*. Issue brief, April 2018. https://www.nationalpartnership.org/our-work/health/reports/black-womens-maternal-health.html.

Neely, Megan Tobias. 2020. "Essential and Expendable: Gendered Labor in the Coronavirus Crisis." Stanford University: Clayman Institute for Gender Research. June 3, 2020. https://gender.stanford.edu/news-publications/gender-news/essential-and-expendable-gendered-labor-coronavirus-crisis.

Petrosky, Emiko, Janet M. Blair, Carter J. Betz, Katherine A. Fowler, Shane P. D. Jack, and Bridget H. Lyons. 2017. "Racial and Ethnic Differences in Homicides of Adult Women and the Role of Intimate Partner Violence—United States, 2003–2014." *Morbidity and Mortality Weekly Report* 66 (28): 741–46.

Reuters. 2020. "UK Tackles Higher Maternal Mortality Rates for Black Mothers." September 15, 2020. https://www.reuters.com/article/uk-britain-health-mothers/uk-tackles-higher-maternal-mortality-rates-for-black-mothers-idUSKBN25T1KM.

Richie, Beth E. 1996. *Compelled to Crime: The Gender Entrapment of Battered Black Women*. New York: Routledge.

Richie, Beth E. 2012. *Arrested Justice: Black Women, Violence, and America's Prison Nation*. New York: New York University Press.

Robertson, Jessica. 2019. "Black Feminism: Looking Back to Move Forward." Unpublished. ResearchGate. Uploaded January 2019. https://www.researchgate.net/publication/330358728.

Santos, Debora de Souza, Mariane de Oliveira Menezes, Carla Betina Andreucci, Marcos Nakamura-Pereira, Roxana Knobel, Leila Katz, Heloisa de Oliveira Salgado, Melania Maria Ramos de Amorim, and Maira L. S. Takemoto. 2021. "Disproportionate Impact of COVID-19 Among Pregnant and Postpartum Black Women in Brazil Through Structural Racism Lens." *Clinical Infectious Diseases* 72 (11): 2067–68.

Sentencing Project. 2020. "Incarcerated Women and Girls." Fact sheet. November 2020. https://www.sentencingproject.org/publications/incarcerated-women-and-girls/.

Stein, Dorit, Kevin Ward, and Catherine Cantelmo. 2020. "Estimating the Potential Impact of COVID-19 on Mothers and Newborns in Low- and Middle-Income Countries." *Health Policy Plus*, April 15, 2020. https://healthpolicyplus.medium.com/estimating-the-potential-impact-of-covid-19-on-mothers-and-newborns-in-low-and-middle-income-3a7887e4a0ff.

Supermajority Education Fund. 2020. "Black Maternal Health Week Highlights COVID-19's Impact on Black Pregnancy." April 14, 2020. https://supermajorityedfund.com/2020/04/black-maternal-health-week-highlights-covid-19s-impact-on-black-pregnancy/.

Taylor, Janette Y. 1998. "Womanism: A Methodologic Framework for African American Women." *Advances in Nursing Science* 21 (1): 53–64.

Turner-Jones, Therese. 2020. "Putting a Stop to Domestic Violence." *Jamaica Observer*, February 16, 2020.

UN-Habitat. 2020. *COVID-19 in African Cities: Impacts, Responses and Poli-cies*. Geneva: UN-Habitat. https://unhabitat.org/sites/default/files/2020/06/covid-19_in_african_cities_impacts_responses_and_policies_2.pdf.

UNICEF and the UN Development Programme. 2020. "Challenges Posed by the COVID-19 Pandemic in the Health of Women, Children, and Adoles-cents in Latin America and the Caribbean." August 2020. https://www.unicef.org/lac/en/reports/challenges-posed-covid-19-pandemic-health-women-children-and-adolescents.

United Nations. n.d. "Explainer: How COVID-19 Impacts Women and Girls: Vi-olence Against Women." Accessed April 2, 2022. https://interactive.unwomen.org/multimedia/explainer/covid19/en/index.html.

Wade, Ashleigh Greene. 2018. "Indigo Child Runnin' Wild: Willow Smith's Ar-chive of Black Girl Magic." In "Black Girl Magic: Gendered Black Politics in the 21st Century," edited by Julia S. Jordan-Zachery with Duchess Harris, special issue, *National Political Science Review* 19 (2): 21–33.

Walker, Alice, 1975. "In Search of Zora Neale Hurston." *Ms.*, March 1975, 74–89.

Walker, Alice. 1983. *In Search of Our Mothers' Gardens: Womanist Prose*. San Diego, Calif.: Harcourt, Brace, Jovanovich.

West, Carolyn M. 2004. "Black Women and Intimate Partner Violence: New Directions for Research." *Journal of Interpersonal Violence* 19 (12): 1487–93.

WorldOMeter. n.d. "Coronavirus Cases." Accessed July 11, 2021. https://www.worldometers.info/coronavirus/#countries.

Young, Daniel. 2020. "Black, Disabled, and Uncounted." National Health Law Pro-gram. August 7, 2020. https://healthlaw.org/black-disabled-and-uncounted/.

CHAPTER 1

#BlackGirlQuarantine Chronicles

On Womanist Artistry, Sisterhood, Survival, and Healing

reelaviolette botts-ward

This piece is an autotheoretical exploration of encounters between selfhood, healing, and care work in 2020.[1] Centering multimedia Black feminist creativity and womanist artistry,[2] I use poetics, prose, and visual art to narrate scenes of intimate exchange among my body, my home, my homegirls, and my healing. From everyday encounters with sister neighbors to virtual sister circles to moments alone in my bathroom, I grapple with themes of safety, protection, refusal, and remorse as I move through an array of emotions that surfaced for me this year.

My diaries are my compass into myself, as they guide me through my processing of grief, loss, and vulnerability. I revisit these diaries, dating from March 1 to December 31, 2020, to journey toward my recollection of 2020 (see figure 1.1). Each journal's 180 pages are filled with marker-colored prose and painted poetics, signed with the sincerity of my attempts to not forfeit my sanity for 2020. I struggled a lot this year—with loss, with work, with "wounds that were never buried deep enough" (botts-ward 2021, 19). This piece is an affirmation of that suffering and a celebration of collective survival. It is a recounting of #BlackGirlQuarantine in the wake of 2020 through the lens of my layered vulnerabilities.[3]

I organize this piece by month to illustrate the progression of pandemonium in my own life and in the collective life of Black womxn in my orbit. Each month's journal entry is a snapshot of the entire 180-paged diary and ends with a creative piece produced between

FIGURE 1.1 The 2020 diaries.

those pages. From sonic healing arts to downtown murals of mourning, Black womxn artists saved me from losing my mind this year. What Black womxn made from the depths of their healing held me close through quarantine. Hence, my making practice, and the creations that inspired it, are the foundation of this work.

I merge my personal creative writing with an academic discourse on racialized and gendered precarity. To make my work legible to broader audiences, I use footnotes as a site of intellectual exchange and allow the body of this text to be read as narrative primarily. My footnotes offer theoretical grounding into intersectional Black feminist scholarship that speaks to my lived and embodied praxis of survival. Bridging works like Alice Walker's *In Search of Our Mothers' Gardens* (1983) with Robin Boylorn's "On Being at Home with Myself: Blackgirl Autoethnography as Research Praxis" (2016), I think about what a homegirl pedagogy of sisterhood looks and feels like in 2020. I argue that this moment of collective grief forces Black womxn to contend with our proximity to precarity in new ways. As our lives

continue to unfold in nuanced form, the pandemic only exacerbates
what we have always known to be true about our vulnerability. Yet,
this moment also affirms what we know to be true about the power of
our own practices of comfort and care for ourselves and one another.

March

Kai hands me a large bottle of hand sanitizer from under her denim
coat, sneaking me the high-priced liquid substance with the subtlety
of a secret, as though making this exchange public could have deadly
effects for the both of us. "You sure?" I asked as I hesitated to hold the
bottle in my hand as my own. If anything, I thought she might need
it more than I. An unhoused Black womxn living at the encampment
on the corner, Kai was much more vulnerable to the coronavirus than
me. I had told her how I'd just come from scouring every drugstore
within a fifty-mile radius of West Oakland and found nothing. The
news kept saying keep sanitizer in yo pocket, but where in the world
was a girl gon' get some from?! Kai leaned in close and whispered,
"Girl, you see that box inside my tent? I'm good!" She pointed to a
large cardboard container with a label that read 50 Piece Sanitizer.
"You take this; I know you gon' need it."

   I was so grateful for her in that moment for having a homegirl
neighbor who shows me what sisterhood feels like in the middle
of a pandemic. As she wiped down all her possessions with bleach-
drenched paper towels, I grabbed a cloth and helped her clean any potential trace of COVID germs from the half-broken wooden dresser.
Kai had her quarantine care plan on lock. She let me know that she
would be "cleanin' and carryin' on" as ritual in this pandemic. The
ethic of care she modeled for the fragments of her homespace, precarious to airborne particles and to the unpredictability of fire that travels
through wind, does not diminish the brutal fact that she is damn tired
of being homeless.[4]

FIGURE 1.2 On behalf of unhoused Black womxn in 2020.

The next week Kai invites me to protest on behalf of Black womxn who live at the encampment. We are demanding that the local motel allow them to stay in vacant rooms since COVID has prevented its normal flow of guests. My sign reads, "Black womxn deserve safe housing in a fuckin pandemic!" (see figure 1.2). The motel refuses, as the owner calls the cops to dissipate the unassuming crowd. They arrive, tell us to go home, and gradually, we do.

I am saddened by the turnout. Nobody came 'cause nobody cared. Unhoused Black folks, and their particular vulnerabilities to the virus, never became central to communal conversations about the layered impacts of this disease. The intersection of race/class/gender/precarity never centered Kai and her needs. The violence of housing insecurity, and the impossibility of shelter in gentrified Oakland, is only exacerbated by this pandemic. The mockery of shelter in place is that Kai, and all my homegirl neighbors who live at the encampment on the corner, wasn't never even sheltered, to begin with.

April

"Corona can't kill the power of Black women's convenings," I say to sixty Black women from across the country Zoomed into my first virtual healing space. The monthly Black womxn's circles that have been going strong on campus for four years are suddenly boxed into my eleven-inch computer screen. My whole life is suddenly boxed into screens, and it seems I might lose myself in them. There is no hand-holding in this virtual circle, no lighting of sage, no textile blankets like we're used to. Just computer screens talking to computer screens, just Black womxn hoping these mediums of surveillance can hold us.[5] As I invite participants to journal on heavy feelings, I write,

Dear daughter of the diaspora / Death is at yo doorstep / How do you respond?[6]

How heavy it is to sit with Black death with such precision. As our mortality looms like dust in the air, we immerse ourselves in a moment of collective grief work to try and gather what is left of our breath. We are exhausted. The whole world is crumbling down around us, and we are expected to hold it together. In this moment, Reanna says, "even the sun feels heavy," and we all feel the same weight. What once soothed our soul now brings us such weight. Braxton wonders what the sun says to the moon when she don't wanna shine. When she just wanna hide. We each map our own social distance between sun and moon, grief and mourning, joy and levity. To try and hold this space with no hands to hold is heavy yet healing (see figure 1.3). Mama here. Sister here. Braxton here. Black womxn who never woulda made it to my healing circle at the University of California, Berkeley, are here. And how good it feels to have my family holding me as I learn to hold this space in a brand-new way.

May

Be careful what window you give into your world. They will find a way to judge you for that. Be careful what you let them see through your

FIGURE 1.3 "Even the sun feels heavy"—Reanna Norman.

screen. They will find a way to judge you for that. Babies calling in for class from shelters. Students judging them for that.

To be forced to merge school and home, work and home, life outside of home forced inside of home (see figure 1.4). And for them to have the nerve to judge you for that. For not having it together on-screen. For not having no screen. For not having access to what you need right now.

I teach a course called Black(Girl) Geographies.[7] We talk about how to make space in our homes, in quarantine, while sheltering in place. How to design the interiors of our home for self-care, how to make a room feel more open, how to force a bedroom to stretch for the sake of our sanity, how to make tight spaces expand in ways that give us more room to breathe. Add a mirror here, declutter a corner there, more floor space, more self-space, more life space (see figure 1.5). Call it Black Feminist Interior Design.[8]

We talk about how sometimes it feels these walls are caving in and how to make home in our bodies when physical sites of comfort are

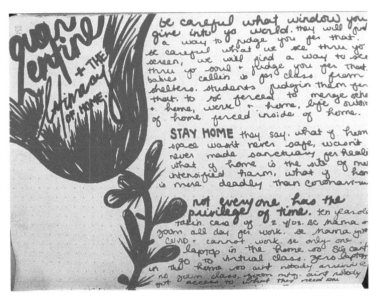

FIGURE 1.4   Quarantine and the intimacy of home.

not afforded (see figure 1.6). When the house is too crowded. When home is unsafe. Stuck in the house that never felt like home with the women and the men who abuse you. Trapped in the house. And the home is the most unsafe space, you know.

We ask, alongside Robin Boylorn's "On Being at Home with Myself" (2016), what it might mean to journey inward toward the self and do the "home work" of self-discovery in the midst of quarantine. What does it mean for a Blackgirl to be stuck at home in 2020?[9]

June

Nowadays, I measure time by the length of my curls. Whether they were blonde or braided or blue. Whether they wrote cursive swirls across my forehead or stayed stuck to themselves beneath bonnets and scarves cuz I couldn't go nowhere no ways. Nowadays my hair don' had a better grasp on reality than me. I began on my natural hair

FIGURE 1.5 A journey inward.

healing journey in quarantine. Been getting to know myself real well, and these curls don' marked my growth.[10]

I learn to mash up molding avocado. Mix it with mayonnaise and honey. Massage it through the meeting of dandruff and kink. With grease and coconut oil. I learn the compass of my scalp, a sacred car-

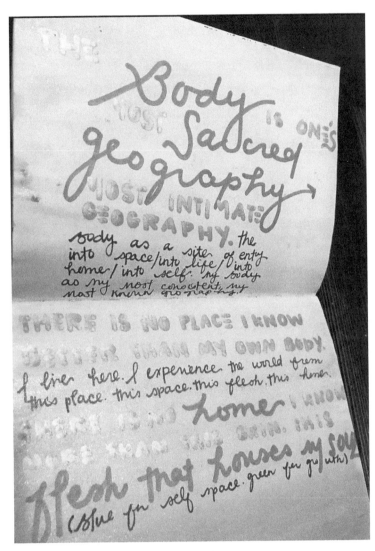

FIGURE 1.6 The body is a sacred geography.

tography of underworlds that brings me close to me. Rearranges the compartments of myself back to me.

When I am in my body, in my head, I return to me more frequently. Return to my senses. Come back to the here and now. How heavy it feels to be standing in a mirror looking like a whole other woman. Re-learning the girl who has tragically stepped into womanhood without warning. Facing whom 2020 made me. Who this year made all of us.

Sat at the stoop of Blackgirl neighbor and learned how to plat and twist. Put in blue braids for protective style. Cover my curls with all the protection I wish I could give to my body. I rename my bathroom *The Spa* and spend time with my body there. With my hair. Stare at myself over and over again to see what I notice, the traces of me I had forgotten. Work to realign the fragmented pieces of my personhood. Place one foot in front of the other. One strand of kink over the other.

I am beginning to feel blue in this season. I see it in my eyes, and I cannot lie. Blue moon. Blue doom. Indigo (see figure 1.7). I listen to Tasha on loop. Same three songs. "The truth is all these rhymes barely hold me together." / "Black girl, we'll leave this fight to someone else for now. You can close your eyes let your hair down." Then Summer Walker, whose album cover is blue. Same three songs about shame and blues. Then Dianna Lopez asks if it's "cold in that world of yours, does it feel blue?" Then Cleo Sol says she is "still cold, still cold, even in [her] home," and I feel that in my bones. I take long hot baths but I still feel cold. Purchase a brand-new fireplace but I still feel cold. Cold as indigo blue. I am a Blackgirl with a bluesoul.[11] That much I know is true.

I braid blue into my scalp like my homegirl taught me. To illustrate Blackgirl bluesoul, to show the incoherence of my youth. I feel free to journey inward in this sea of blue. I paint a picture of myself and I name it Blue. Deep blue hair like deep blue waves. Deep blue braids that shimmer even in the shade. Look what I made on my scalp. A self sanctuary I am proud of.

FIGURE 1.7 Indigo Blues. This diary entry quotes Lupe Fiasco's "WAV Files" (2018), where he states, "My bones is why the beach is white, Why the beach is white 'cause they bleached us light, So I'm goin' back home, I took a leap last night, So I'm walkin' on water 'til my feet just like Jesus Christ, Wow, walkin' on water, Wow, wow, walkin' on water."

July

I walk downtown Oakland to yell #SAYHERNAME in a crowd full of folks I don't know. My homegirl buys me a #BlackLivesMatter mask cuz I rushed out of the house and forgot mines. We march and we yell and demand to be seen/heard/felt. We march past Black womxn raised on stilts painting brick walls Black. Black as the harm and the healing that we dance between. Painting faces of forgotten and missing onto boarded-up buildings. Black girls standin' on boxes. Making protest signs out of cardboard boxes. Whole hood painted hella Black. That we would risk our lives to protest for our lives shows the level of urgency in this fight. Whole city on fire for four whole nights, and still, we're in the streets for this fight. Oakland becomes a Black mother who holds us close in our grief, who gives our bodies the space we need to mourn.

I am teaching a class called Black Feminist Healing Arts. My first lecture is on Black womxn's precarity in 2020. I ask if anyone has heard of Oluwatoyin Salau.[12] A student asks, "is that the story about the lynching?" I say no, there were five separate stories of Black people being lynched in the past few weeks but this is not that. This is a story of a young Black woman who died a different brutal way. To speak about lynching in present tense, to teach a class of Black and brown womxn about lynching in the present tense—the eeriness of it left me in tears. We listened to Noname's "Song 33" and cried together about how unprotected our Black womxnhood be. "I saw a demon on my shoulder, it's lookin' like patriarchy . . . Why Toyin body don't embody all the life she wanted? A baby, just nineteen." The Black girl students in class echo, "I'm just nineteen, I'm just nineteen. I protest in these streets, it could've happened to me."

I encourage my students to connect with inner creativity as a Black feminist praxis, to reclaim pieces of our power, to express and release remnants of that weight. I realize that I must do so, too. I pick up the hook and the stitch again. Crochet myself a crop top. Present my final creative project alongside my students'. My sister and mother join our Zoom room as special guest presenters who have something to say about Black girlhood and making. I am honored to center the womxn in my family in academic knowledge production. Our intergenerational womanist art praxis becomes a rigorous site of analysis (see figure 1.8). My mother and my sister become scholars worthy of citation.[13]

August

There is a sadness in my eyes that can be seen on-screen. A weight of unwellness in the aftermath of loss piled on loss that is lingering. A

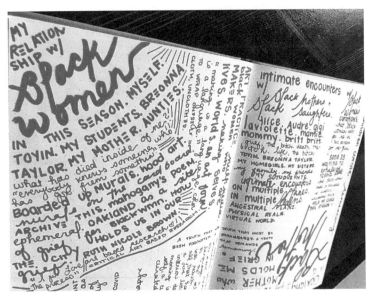

FIGURE 1.8 Black mothers, Black daughters, and grieving.

heaviness in being unhealed. There is a somber, unsoothed sensation stuck in my throat. A weariness trapped to my chest. Shallow breaths. And the sky is burning.[14] I feel unheld. Unhealed. Unwell. And I will not say why because I do not think I know, but 2020 has had its hold on me. There is a sorrow that is as dark as the orange moon that motions for my sanity in the noontime. It is Wednesday and it is dark and it is only twelve p.m. I am way too sad to be on Zoom today. There is no sun today. There is no sun today. The whole world's on fire and I need sun today. But there's no sun today. I got none today.

I miss the wind on my face. The sun on my cheek. The dirt under my toenails. The rocks at the creek. I miss the subtle movement of dandelion flowers at my doorstep. How yellow butterflies would dance between moons.

I miss my stoop. I made them three stairs at the front of my home a portal into my past/present/future. Made that stoop my playground. My ancestral recall. My altar. My healing space. From that stoop I would go to all the places I ever loved at once and reside still in that moment. I would be all the parts of me I never learned to love and reside right there in a moment.

and COVID came
and i was stuck inside
but i always had *my stoop.*
and then protests came
and it was not safe
but i always had *my stoop.*
then the heat wave came
then the fires came
and they took away
my stoop. the one space
i had to cover me
was stolen from me
by the wind
because i could not breathe
with fire in the air

This summer I rediscovered my love for rocks as I sat with Sobonfu Somé's *Spirit of Intimacy* (1997, 47). "Rocks mean . . . our ability to re-member." As I recalled my childhood practice of collecting rocks from the schoolyard, I lined my windowsill with stones I collected from the lake, from the stream, from the ocean. I sat beneath those channels of memory and opened up my spirit to that which had been forgot-ten—my power, my peace, my harmony. This summer I allowed Black feminism to invite me back to me. Became bold and unapologetic in my womanish womanist manifesto. Crocheted and reconnected with my mother and her mother. Learned to slow down in the middle of the pandemic. To not rush myself. My work. My healing. Found free-dom in the wind. Felt moved, deeply, by how Black women love Black women, and how Black women who love Black women love me. Became creative. Curious. Youthful again. This was a spiritual summer, and my stoop was my sanctuary for this season.

As a woman learning to love herself through nature, losing outside felt devastating. For a woman finding herself for the first time, between the calming of a stream, a rock, a lake, the tree, a breeze through trees, not having access to nature felt debilitating. I was learning to feel for the first time because rocks reminded me of my humanity. Outside was the one thing I had left to keep me grounded, and somehow god managed to take that from me too. I was angry. I had finally found my morning routine. Wake. Wander through marble cabinets for honey-scented tea. Make myself two cups. Sit on my stoop and sit with the sun and remind myself that I am human. Draw and paint and color and play and try my best to be present. We are in a pandemic but I still have myself. I still have my home. I still have the sun and outdoors. Two, three, four hours would pass, and I would not stop till class time. Draw. Color. Paint on repeat. Creating so I could stay sane. The journal itself became my most sacred site of care work, and the stoop the location from which I convened with all the parts of me that unfolded and unraveled into my diary.

And now the sun is gone. And now the wind is gone. And it is hot in my house. I am breaking out. The air is not clean. I cannot breathe. I am sheltered in place. Outside is not safe. Inside is not safe. There is nowhere to escape. The heat wave. The fires. The smoke. The police. The pandemic. Nowhere to go. Everything closed. We are never able to breathe (see figure 1.9).

Summer stretched from March to August in 2020. And this is how my summer ends. Numb. Closed windows. Never enough air to breathe. Stuck. Trapped. Sulking. Mourning the me I never got to meet, grieving the self I never got to be. Time ran out in summer 2020. Time ran out on me. And this is how the summer ends. With loose ends. With regret. About all the things that never got to happen. The trips we never got

FIGURE 1.9 A world on fire.

to take. The memories we never got to make. The rest that never came. The reset that never came. The fall bleeds into the summer. The summer bleeds into the fall. I have no sense of time.

September

This screen holds the residue of every encounter, compiles the energy of every interaction I have had since quarantine. Every moment a silent intruder spent in sacred space must be saged away. I sage down my mouse, and every other ounce of unsafety still lingering on this laptop.

Virtual violation of sacred space takes its toll on a Blackgirl spirit. When you do all you can to make space safe and you can't 'cause you Black and womxn and don't nobody give a fuck about protecting you. And you do all you can do to protect you. Protect Black girls. Protect Black womxn. But there is nothing you can do to ensure that no harm will come to you. Facing the weight of virtual vulnerability. Exposure to harm maps onto the Zoom room.

Unsafe in my own body. Unsafe in my own home. Anyone can do anything to me and nobody will do nothing about it. Anyone can do anything to us and nobody will do nothing about it. Breonna Taylor. Oluwatoyin Salau. Dominique Fells. &&& . . . I am too tired to fight for me. I am too tired to fight for us. I just wish someone would fight for me. Fight for we. Fight for us. I am worthy of protection. But I ain't got the strength to keep fighting for the protection that is owed to me. I am heavy. Weary from this weight. Unsafe. Unsafe. It is always unsafe.

My sisters catch me. Invite me to write about pedagogy and praxis for an article on academia and healing.[15] Meet twice a month and hold one another through the phone. Through the screen. Teach me it is possible to receive love from here. I find joy and peace in the proximity to closeness that I feel in the midst of the distance forced on us. The isolation we ain't never been accustomed to. But in this process of putting a paper together, we come closer than we've ever been. We are naming this sister circle as a method for our research, but really it is a tool for our survival. We did not even notice that in writing in community as praxis, we were alchemizing the care work we each needed to give and receive in this season.

And then we have a slumber party. With homegirls, sisters, and friends. Social distanced. Masks on. But in one another's presence for the first time. It felt so good to not be alone in my home, drowning in the fear of harm that my dreams told me would come to me. It hurt to not be able to hug, but still, I felt so held.

We talk about inner child healing. About all the little brown girl inside needs to feel safe again. How triggered she has been by this new normal that we refuse to accept as normal. This business-as-usual attitude that's been projected onto us. How antiBlackwoman it is to expect us to show up in the ways we always have when the whole world is falling apart. And how much pressure that puts on the little girl inside us, who is trying her best to be well. "I'm tryna do

FIGURE 1.10 My best is based on my capacity.

my best, but my best is based on my capacity! Right now I am still recovering, so like, I really don't have the capacity!" My girls affirmed
me and reminded me, "Nothing matters more than your wellness,
sis. Nothing matters more than your healing" (see figures 1.10, 1.11,
and 1.12).

FIGURE 1.11 There is nothing more urgent than my healing.

October

There are sisters on both sides. The two my mother had and the three her mother had. There is an intergenerational gap between the girls who were born between 1960 and the Detroit riots, and the ones who were born into Bush. Misunderstandings about motherhood, sisterhood, and family ties, about legacy, lineage, and remembering. I feel, at times, a silence in my naming of *sister*, an unrelenting rejection of the weight of it. All that it carries. All it requires. All that it makes known. There is a weight to being blood.

There is one way to say *sister* and mean the women who you love, with whom you do not share a mother. And then there is a naming of sister that is more heavy. More loving, and yet, at times, more tangled. At times congested in the mucus of my yearning. At times I wonder why women with the same mother and the same childhood home see things so differently.

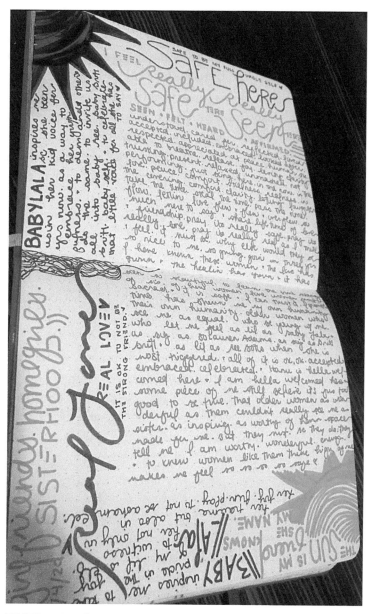

FIGURE 1.12 Safety in sisterhood.

In 2020, I sat with the word *sister* and all its multiple meanings. In moments when Auntie Cherie called a Zoom date in the group chat, and we danced to Stevie Wonder, singing off-key, sipping wine and sparkling cider, making stuck at home feel real good. Celebrating our first reconvening in six whole years, how pandemic brought us together. I think about the meaning of *sister* when Auntie Mickey plans a surprise virtual gathering for Mama's birthday, featuring a slideshow of pigtails and afros, pictures of my mother in seventh grade skating through Detroit alleyways, pictures of prom queens and pressed-out perms.

I love the generations of sisters. The way we say *La Violette Girls* in sync, conjuring my mother's maiden name, the name she once shared with her sisters. The way we women of this bloodline show up for sister/daughter/niece and blur the terms at our convenience. How my sister pretends she is a sister to my mother, and not a daughter, acting real womanish, playing Auntie homegirl and dressing up with grown folks as if she were twice her age. How "we three twins" becomes a call for connectivity between my mother, my sister, and me. I love the love poured into the memory of home—Detroit, Atlanta, Philadelphia—the nostalgia I develop for places I never knew. I love the laughter about yellow tank tops and whitewashed jeans, about whose hair stood the highest and why "mama wouldn't let Gigi get no fro," first dates, first kiss, and sneaking out the back do'. I love the memory of my mother from another time, I love the power of memory most in these times, in times when we cannot be close.

I fly to Philadelphia to be with my childhood home before it is sold, and my mother will not hug me. Do you know how heavy a feeling it is to fly cross-country and not settle into the arms of a mother's embrace? My mother could not hug me. COVID. Social distance. I fly cross-country to D.C. to see Auntie Mickey outside the forty minutes allotted for the Zoom room and she tells me she can only see me through the Zoom room. Do you know how heavy it is to not hug anyone you love, to not see the women you love beyond Zoom rooms?

I think about the meaning of *sister* when my mother's oldest daughter stays up past four a.m., her time, to help me insert box braids into my scalp with a FaceTime live tutorial. Me in California, my sister in Atlanta. How we work to close the distance, in the midst of COVID, through screens. And when the screens are not enough, how we hop on planes and fly cross-country to hold each other close through quarantine. To assist with curls and baby hair swirls. With braids and bangs and the latest fashion craze. In the moments when my sister becomes my mother and feeds me warmth, makes a space for me in her new home. No return date. No return flight. A one way and I don't know when I will leave but I need this closeness, this energy. Even if it is socially distanced (see figure 1.13).

There is an impossibility of familial intimacy. A gap between baby child and her mother. A mother and her sisters. There is no way for

FIGURE 1.13 Rolling waves of lonely.

us to do what women do in convenings. To hold one another long enough to rock the fear away. To know you are safe in the arms of the woman who cradles your wounds in her womb. An urgent restructuring of cultural care, communal comfort, collective concern. There is no way to mourn without my mother's love. I am longing for the touch of her, the scent of her, a glimpse into the turquoise of her shimmer, a subtle notice of the tiny mole beneath her cheek. You must be closer than six feet to notice these things. I am forced to be far away. We got some deep deep dark dark healing to do, and we are forced to be so far away. I cannot heal if I cannot touch you. I need to hold you and know it's real.

There are six feet between us. My mother, my sister, and me. And six feet between them, my mother and my aunties who I cannot see. We do not step into the world with one another. We only walk with emoji figures of ourselves across a screen that is suffocating the entirety of our lives. My eyes hurt. My heart hurts. This brings me pain. Bizarre and bewildering pain. To pretend not to need all six of our feet in step with one another. What brings us together keeps us apart. How can we heal when existing in a reality that is mediated by the absence of touch?

November

Braxton died. I cannot believe that Braxton died. I refuse to accept that Braxton died on November the second at twenty-one years old. I cannot comprehend the levels of grief we have known in 2020. Seems like everybody I know don' lost somebody. It was only a matter of time before I was next in line to lose somebody. All year, I kept holding my breath with that lingering anxiety. Who is next, who will be next? This proximity to death lingering. But never did I ever think it would be baby girl. Never did I ever imagine it would be Braxie.

There are three sisters on both sides. The three her mother had, and the three her mother's mother had. Heavy. How both sets of sisters lost a sister in 2020. How her mama mourned her baby sister and her baby child six months apart. Heavy. How I watch my little sister mourn her baby sister. How the crying I cannot bring myself to do haunts me.

Everyone, everywhere, is tweeting about Brax.[16] Her face plastered 'cross every media screen. Young rapper. Twenty-one years old. Beloved. Unapologetic Black femme glory. Radical Black dyke energy. Larger than life to so many, but to me she was my little sister's little sister.

The funeral services are heavy and hard. Everyone wearing masks and you do not know exactly who is crying beneath that cloth. How heavy it is. To mourn a little sister in 2020.

I loved her because she was not afraid of herself. She never turned away from herself. She remained so brave and so bold in her healing. She visits me in this realm from where she now resides and I cry. And I cry. And I cry. But still there is water that gets choked up, in my throat, and I am unable to release. I dedicate the next healing circle to Braxie, and we cry and we cry about how much baby girl changed all our lives—her fans, her friends, her sisters (see figures 1.14, 1.15, and 1.16).

December

I had my first panic attack on an airplane with a mask on. Could not breathe. Hyperventilating. It was everything. Just everything crashing down on me. The weight of the world in 2020. The loss and grief. The precarity that is ongoing.

My partner is in a car accident and I have to get home but we cannot deboard the plane. I have to get home, I cannot miss the next plane.

FIGURE 1.14 Orange moon, inspired by Erykah Badu.

This layover can't keep me from getting home. I need to go home. I am so heavy and I need to be home. I lose my sanity at the thought of not making it home to my husband, who might die at any moment.

They hold the plane for me. I sprint across the airport and pass out on the plane. A Black woman flight attendant, who does not know

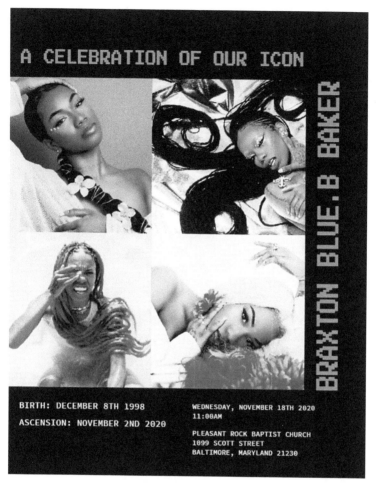

FIGURE 1.15 Braxton Blue B. Baker's obituary, by Courtney Lett.

my name, brings me water and asks me what I need to be well. I am held in her capacity to see me. Through the mask. Through the fall. In my loss of breath. It was everything. Everything. The looming of precarity in this season.

Six feet apart. Six feet under. Social distance. So much space. Such a gaping hole in my chest. Watching Black womxn who know me most

FIGURE 1.16   Braxton loves orange.

be unable to hold me. Watching Black womxn way too young go six feet under. Six feet apart. Six feet under.

I have been meeting my inner[blackgirl]child gradually in 2020 (see figure 1.17).[17] The more I lean in, the more she comes out. *Hi, my name is Britt Britt* (see figure 1.18). Me and Braxton spoke about inner child healing as Black womxn with Black girls inside us. Braxton died, and my inner child came out like never before. Hurt. Sad. Angry. Mad. Why do Black girls always gotta die? She wants to know. She needs to understand why she is always so unsafe.

We spent much of 2020 creating art together (see figure 1.19). She returned me to creativity, and following her lead, I found grounding in the practice of creating something beautiful for myself. Ten jour-

FIGURE 1.17 Pretty brown girl—by Britt Britt and me.

FIGURE 1.18 Baby phat, baby gurl—by Britt Britt and me.

nals to show for our journey through 2020. Toni Cade Bambara (1980, 1) says, "a lot of weight when you're well," and I feel that wholeheartedly. This year has been so much weight, but we have been working to be well. Together. Britt Britt and me. She has taught me how to hold me close through all the chaos of this season. She has shown me how to love more abundantly.

FIGURE 1.19 Ancestors holding me.

Notes

1. According to the Association for the Study of the Arts of the Present, as described in its *ASAP/Journal* call for papers on autotheory, an autotheoretical approach "moves between the worlds of 'theory' and 'practice,' often exceeding disciplinary boundaries, genres, and forms." In conversation with my "Healing at Home: on Self Making and Black Girl Interiors" (botts-ward 2022), I frame autotheory as a tool for merging the personal and the theoretical to provide nuanced insight into the specificity of my lived experience, amid the broader structural implications of Black women's heightened vulnerabilities in 2020. I wrote "Healing at Home" years before quarantine, and I view this piece as an expansion of my earlier work. This moment forced me to reimagine what healing at home looks like in times of global crisis. Thus, leaning into autotheory allows me to process personal injury in the context of collective suffering.

2. Grounded in Alice Walker's definition of womanism from *In Search of Our Mothers' Gardens* (1983), I frame womanism here as the creative process by which Black women make life beautiful in the midst of ongoing vulnerability. I place Black feminist creativity and womanist artistry in conversation with each other to draw on both genealogies of thought to center radical life-making processes of Black women.

3. #BlackGirlQuarantine is a term I use to refer to the layered gendered and racialized violences Black womxn and girls encountered from March to December 2020 as extensions of the normative violences experienced before COVID-19. I use this term in conversation with #BlackGirlQuarantine: An Exhibition of #BlackWomxnHealing in the Wake of 2020, a virtual exhibition that I hosted in Spring 2021, with funding by the University of California's Arcus Endowment. This exhibition was inspired by my encounters with Black womxn, who returned me to the power of artistry in the midst of global catastrophe. It is housed on my virtual platform for Black feminist digital humanities, Black Womxn Healing (https://blackwomxnhealing.com).

4. In *Chocolate Cities: A Black Map of American Life*, Marcus Anthony Hunter and Zandria F. Robinson (2018, 33) assert that "Black mapping [frames] . . . how Black people make place in response to and critique [of] . . . gentrification processes." Kai and the community of unhoused Black womxn who live at this encampment map their own geographic process of refusal onto the landscape of the gentrified city in the midst

of the pandemic, and demand that the city create safety for them. Yet, there remains an impossibility of housing and the institutional neglect that makes this precarity a reality.

5. In *Dark Matters: On the Surveillance of Blackness*, Simone Browne (2015) writes about the violence of surveillance through various technological forms. Her text provides a useful framework for theorizing the impossibilities of virtual safety in 2020.

6. In "A Wake Work for 2020: On Meeting Black Grief with Tenderness," I write with colleague Osceola Ward (2020), in conversation with Christina Sharpe's *In the Wake: on Blackness and Being* (2016), about the ongoing realities of Black death and suffering, and about how Black death mapped onto 2020 is a continuation of the gratuitous violence we Black folks experience in the afterlife of enslavement.

7. Black(Girl) Geographies is an undergraduate course that I designed to support students' reading and writing abilities through the study of Blackness, womanhood, space making, and home.

8. In my dissertation, "I See You, Sis: Curations of Black Women's Healing Spaces in Oakland" (in progress), I coin Black Feminist Interior Design as a process of self making and home making that occurs in the physical and metaphysical realms simultaneously. I argue that as Black women design the interiors of our home, we curate an interiority of the self that expands possibilities of self-care and creative healing.

9. Boylorn's groundbreaking methodological intervention results in an innovative research praxis, entitled Blackgirl autoethnography, that invites Black women researchers to center our relationship to body, home, and interiority in the process of data collection. Building on the work of canonical Black feminist ethnographers like Zora Neale Hurston and Katherine Dunham, Boylorn (2016, 44) refuses to divorce herself from the work and argues that she is, in fact, part of the work to be done, as her methodology is designed for "black women to do the home/work of self-construction." She offers a theoretically rich analysis of Black feminist home making as she journeys into herself and her homes to make sense of her own interiority. Her use of Blackgirl autoethnography and her framing of homespace curation provide foundational tools for my own healing, and for my intellectual analysis of Blackgirl homespace in 2020.

10. In "PsychoHairapy: Using Hair as an Entry Point into Black Women's Spiritual and Mental Health," Afiya Mbilishaka (2018) points to the ther-

apeutic relationship between Black women and hair. She argues that Black women's hair care has the transformative potential to enhance our self-care and our overall psychological well-being. I think here alongside Mbilishaka about the power of my hair-care journey in quarantine and the way that connecting with my natural hair journey invited me more deeply into self-care.

11. In *mourning my inner[black/girl]child* (2021), I write about the relationship between Black girlhood and sadness, using bluesoul to name the despair and darkness I was forced to know in my youth. The lyrics in the text are quoted from, respectively, Tasha, "But There's Still the Moon" (2020); Tasha, "Lullaby" (2018); Summer Walker, "Shame" (2018); Dianna Lopez, "Blu" (2019); and Cleo Sol, "Still Cold" (2016).

12. Oluwatoyin "Toyin" Salau "was a 19 year old activist from Tallahassee, Florida. Toyin, described as 'powerful and strong with a happy soul' was a fierce advocate for the full protection of Black lives." Toyin's body was found on June 15, 2020, in Tallahassee, after she released "a series of tweets describing sexual assault" (Justice for Black Girls, n.d.). The organization Justice for Black Girls created the Freedom Fighter's Fund in honor of Toyin, to support Black girl activists with basic needs. As of June 2021, the fund had awarded a total of $75,000 to over fifty Black girls activists. Through initiatives like these, Toyin's legacy lives on.

13. Alice Walker's *In Search of Our Mothers' Gardens* (1983, 239) became a primary course text. Her use of womanism as a sacred spiritual art form, and her centering of mothers, became the foundation of praxis we attempted to embody in the course. Bringing my mother to my class was an attempt to bridge the gap between two worlds, an effort to make real the claim that I do this work for our mothers. Centering my mother's creative practice, alongside my sister's, provided an opportunity to see the everyday nature of womanist artistry, a language for theorizing the mundane ways that we Black womxn curate a life for ourselves.

14. Between July 24 and December 12, 2020, the entire state of California, and its surrounding states, suffered from one of the worst wildfire seasons in history. Even when fires were counties away, the residue of smoke could be felt from my doorstep in Oakland. For months, it was extremely unsafe to step outside because breathing the toxic air was damaging to the lungs. The air was contaminated with particles of burned-up buildings and decimated homes from far-off cities, and pieces of the torn-apart hopes and dreams from people who had lost everything.

15.   This article is now forthcoming from the *Journal of Educational Foundations* (botts-ward, Reynolds, and Pour-Khorshid, forthcoming).

16.   Braxton Blue B. Baker (@dykebrax on Instagram) was an iconic Black queer artist whose music, fashion, and healing arts unaopologetically centered Blackness, dykism, womxnhood, and healing. Upon her passing, a global network of fans expressed an outpouring of gratitude for her life's work. To learn more about the legacy of her artistry, visit the website Brax Blue.B Legacy (https://braxlegacy.com).

17.   My first book, *mourning my inner[black/girl]child* (2021) explores the relationship between Black womxn and our inner Black girl. I argue that inner child healing for Black womxn is a process of reclamation that centers the racialized and gendered harms we experienced in our youth. Through reconnecting with childhood memories and youthful nostalgia, I have come to hear the voice of the little girl in me who is longing for the love, care, comfort, and protection that she never received. In 2020, she has been my most cherished guide, leading me back to me.

References

Bambara, Toni Cade. 1980. *The Salt Eaters*. New York: Random House.

botts-ward, reelaviolette. 2021. *mourning my inner[black/girl]child*. Oakland, Calif.: Nomadic Press.

botts-ward, reelaviolette. 2022. "Healing at Home: On Self Making and Black Girl Interiors." *ASAP/J*, March 18, 2022. https://asapjournal.com/transmedial -autotheories-5-healing-at-home-on-self-making-and-black-girl-interiors -ree-botts/.

botts-ward, reelaviolette, Aja D. Reynolds, and Farima Pour-Khorshid. Forthcoming. "Breaking Cycles: Curating a Woman of Color Feminist Praxis of Spiritual Reclamation in the Academy." *Journal of Educational Foundations*.

botts-ward, reelaviolette, and Osceola Ward. 2020. "A Wake Work for 2020: On Meeting Black Grief with Tenderness." *Root Work Journal* 1 (1). https://doi .org/10.47106/111104774.

Boylorn, Robin. 2016. "On Being at Home with Myself: Blackgirl Autoethnography as Research Praxis." *International Review of Qualitative Research* 9 (1): 44–58.

Browne, Simone. 2015. *Dark Matters: On the Surveillance of Blackness*. Durham, N.C.: Duke University Press.

Cleo Sol. 2018. "Still Cold." *Winter Songs*. Forever Living Originals. EP and digital download.

Hunter, Marcus Anthony, and Zandria F. Robinson. 2018. *Chocolate Cities: The Black Map of American Life*. Berkeley: University of California Press.

Justice for Black Girls. n.d. "Freedom Fighter's Fund." Accessed April 2, 2022. https://www.justiceforblackgirls.com/programs/freedom-fighters-fund.

Lopez, Dianna. 2019. "Blu." Single. Written by Dianna Lopez and Aren Flower. Digital download.

Lupe Fiasco. 2018. "WAV Files." *Drogas Wave*. 1st and 15th Productions. Digital download.

Mbilishaka, Afiya. 2018. "PsychoHairapy: Using Hair as an Entry Point into Black Women's Spiritual and Mental Health." *Meridians* 16 (2): 382–92.

Noname. 2020. "Song 33." Single. Digital download.

Sharpe, Christina. *In the Wake: On Blackness and Being*. Durham, NC: Duke University Press, 2016.

Somé, Sobonfu. 1997. *The Spirit of Intimacy: Ancient African Teachings in the Ways of Relationships*. Berkeley, Calif.: Berkeley Hills Books.

Tasha. 2018. "Lullaby." *Alone at Last*. Father/Daughter Records, FD-078. Digital download.

Tasha. 2020. "But There's Still the Moon." Single. Father/Daughter Records, FD-094. Digital download.

Walker, Alice. 1983. *In Search of Our Mothers' Gardens: Womanist Prose*. San Diego, Calif.: Harcourt, Brace, Jovanovich.

Walker, Summer. 2018. "Shame." *Last Day of Summer*. LVRN and Interscope Records. Digital download.

CHAPTER 2

Advanced Directive and Lessons Learned on the Battlefield

Brianna Y. Clark

Precious Lord, take my hand
Lead me on, let me stand
I am tired, I am weak, I am worn
Through the storm, through the night
Lead me on through the light

—Thomas A. Dorsey, "Take My Hand, Precious Lord"

Rustic oak trees, interspersed with knee-high small spiny prickly pear cacti, are part of the landscape of this ancient resting place. Oak trees offer a smooth, calming scent, a scent that is expansive over the wide-open southwest Texas terrain that engulfs me with a sense of being and presence. It is a natural smooth tree musk complemented by the sound of soft rustling leaves. The cemetery in the rolling hills of southwest Texas where these trees and cacti grow is also where my ancestors live. The cemetery is peacefully resting in a space separated from traffic lights and city illumination. Down the road a few miles from the cemetery, you'll find a football stadium sitting on the eastern edge of a major university built around an old plantation. My ancestors' hands built that plantation, and the university, too. Cemeteries are among the best history and science textbooks available; they tell stories unsung by victors. The cemetery is old. It used to be the Negro cemetery, a cemetery of the "other." A cemetery for those different enough to be placed on unwanted land but similar enough to require traditional burial. When blatant segregation was no longer in vogue, it became a paupers' cemetery.

My family would drop by this almost forgotten cemetery hidden at the far end of unkempt roads, behind weather-aged single-wide trailers, when I was younger. We would arrive at the cemetery before college football games to respect our elders and remember who we are. Dressed in my spirited maroon and gold collegiate gear, I was always pulled in by the peacefulness of the oak trees, the scent that magically lingered, the hard weather-tested concrete of tombstones, and the small cacti that I diligently avoided tripping over. When I was a child, it was a place where the hustle and cheering of a small southern college town gave way to the timeless call-and-response of my ancestors' plea to God: *Precious Lord, take my hand.* History is present in this place, blurring the lines between the past, present, and future. From a child's eye, my perspective of the kings and queens who have taken their rest in this hallowed place was limited by my inability to grasp the depth of their pain and despair. My grade school education never touched on this part of history. My grade school education didn't offer adequate or accurate historical context. This cemetery held often-hidden histories; it held lessons on battlefield survival for the Black feminist. The cemetery is a record of resistance displayed in concrete, granite, and marble. A resistance unsung by white history.

⸺   ⸺

Prickly pear cacti are interesting plants; their spines create a nervelike sharp pain that pierces the soul when touched. *Lead me on, let me stand.* When the spines of a cactus are burned away, the oblong pad of the cactus feels soft and almost rubbery with the sense that there is unknown nourishment with a healing substance beneath it. Cacti have edible nourishment that generations before knew had health and healing benefits that have only recently been rediscovered by the hipsters and in-crowd on the university campus. From a distance, the general soft light-green smoothness of the cactus almost makes you forget about the intense pain awaiting if there is contact. The cacti are familiar enough to be a piece of the natural flora, but their touch is painful enough to evoke generations of painful memories and flash-backs. *I am weak, I am worn.*

Once, while craftily dodging fledgling cacti by using the tops of worn-down tombstones as support, I noticed the over-recurring date of 1918 carved into stone. A repeated death date. *Through the storm, through the night.* Infants, toddlers, twentysomethings, and the elderly alike all shared a common finality. As we drove away from the cemetery to our greater Texas ritual of pregame tailgating, I began to ask my parents why 1918. The transition from the peaceful ancestral space where I was one of many to the university campus awakened a sense of loss and questioning of what led us to this point, an existential crisis at an age when I didn't have words to describe what I was feeling. What was the meaning of my life and those lives so briefly described on the tombstones?

Even as a child, I knew life was hard for many people at the turn of the century, and it was especially tough for Black people. I had a general sense of historical facts without the context and depth of truly knowing accounts of our ancestral past. Listening to my older relatives' routine conversations about doctors' appointments and health insurance forms gave insight into the lack of access and struggle to do more with less. Much as it is today, in the early 1900s, there was poor health-care access, systemic racism, and the presumption that those with darker skin are guilty until proven innocent. Yet, I did not understand why the tombstones were telling a chilling story of life that just ended in 1918. Eventually, I would learn of the Spanish flu.

I don't recall the football game that day, a sin unforgivable in the greater Texas tradition, but I recall the feeling of total loss and the thankfulness that 1918 would never happen again. It was a historical event, a case study in history. It would become a familial case study on the survival of Black women experiencing racial disparities. My mother used it as a teaching point to make my sister and me aware that we came from a strong line of Black women. These were Black women who worked through an unfair, unequal environment littered with death and loss to bring us to where we are today. *Lead me on through the light.*

There are lessons learned from the deaths of 1918, lessons about perseverance, injustice of life, and the value of knowledge, generational knowledge. I learned about perseverance from my great-great-grandmother Johanna Hardeman—an independent farmer, a position acquired by unknown familial relationships—and the lack of business partnership afforded to Black women during the early 1900s. She is buried in that cemetery along with generations proceeding her. She was a hard-working Black woman who relied on the land for subsistence. No government programs provided safety nets for poor Black landowners, especially Black women. Though Black people were forced to pay taxes, agricultural extension agencies were not interested, nor required by law, to provide help, unless the land was owned by white people and sharecropped by Black people. My mother always told my sister and me that we had no reason ever to give up. If Johanna could do what she did with such limited resources, how dare we limit ourselves because the world isn't fair or as planned? Working for the land teaches many lessons, from the need for patience and consistency to the reliance on science. It requires early mornings of persistence, believing that science will come through, transforming seeds into nourishment.

Farming is an act of resistance and faith that a forgettable seed will become something lifesaving when given the gift of time and attention. Although I chose a health-care career, the familial lessons of farming have prepared me for who I am today and who I am in this current pandemic—1918 becomes merged with 2020. I've learned persistence and faith in the process of change and the ability for regeneration. In the same way that rested soil brings a stronger yield, I have found, the human body reflects the same behavior. Both are strong and resilient but can be harmed beyond repair by natural and man-made forces. It is possible to scorch the earth beyond any repair; it is also possible to damage a person's relationship with the health-care system to the point that all faith in the system is lost.

We are left with the questions of what lessons are learned and how we sustain ourselves. The reality is that there is no quick resolution. Black people are being asked to fix a problem that we did not create; we are the victims of a situation forced on us. Being female, Black, and poor in 1918 meant that injustice was a part of life; no gunslinging hero was riding in to save the day. The rugged fair-skinned cowboy riding off into the sunset after a hard day's work is a legend for text-books. Our story sharply contradicts the textbook narrative. Being female, Black, and poor in the new millennium means that terror is a part of life. There is no marvelous superhero to swoop in and save the day. We are left with our faith, our faith that hope still grows in the long-forgotten concreted-over fields. Life was not charming then, and it is lived now on the battlefield of dreams and passions dissi-pated. The only justice to counter the injustice was to keep living to the best of your ability and believing that there were better days ahead. Black women learned to till the soil they were given. The only peace to counter terror is to push forward, believing that with time and pressure, concrete gives way to will at its weakest points.

The gift of ancestral knowledge has proven more valuable than the land we worked on. Ancestral knowledge has shown us a path through the pandemic perils; it has proven to be the unexpected peace in the eye of the storm. Our ancestral knowledge is the furnace show-ing us that our bootstraps were never there to support us; weaker than the fire, the bootstraps were never for us. Land ownership has and continues to be the prized asset in American culture, the phys-ical manifestation of blood, sweat, and tears. Through hard lessons

learned, land can be bought, sold, and stolen through legal and illegal avenues. However, knowledge of the past, the present, and our
surroundings is something that can never be stolen. Whether it was
learned in the fields or in a classroom, education is and has always
been a cornerstone to our progress forward.

The lessons taught to me about managing a farm in a world stacked
against us have taught me more about the American health-care system than any classroom lecture. I've learned that even the most organized and prepared poor Black woman can still fail in our medical
system. Faith is all we have; sometimes, the discarded squash seeds in
the trash pile grow better than those in the field. Johanna has personally taught me more about policy, decision-making, and the leverag-
ing of health options than I could have ever realized as a child. Her
story has helped me process the layers of pain and despair that thrive
in the health-care system. Analysis aside, faith is all I have. Faith that
the least racist doctor stands behind that exam door. Faith that the
hospital's policy was written with a poor Black woman in mind. Faith
that hope survives on a battlefield paved with concrete.

Fast-forwarding to today, I see that I was wrong about the finality of
the pandemic of 1918. Being a Black woman during the Spanish flu was
a primer for us all. It was a training course on Black feminism and the
American health-care system, teaching us the meaning of recognizing
the value in ourselves and our lives. As a health-care professional, I
have watched Black women struggle with social and health-care access,
living in fear that their steps through the entry of a health-care facility
may be their last. I constantly worry about my fellow Black women
receiving fair treatment in health clinics in America. In society, per-
ception is everything; the old comfy sweatpants that the human body
welcomes during a viral cold as the sentinel sign for illness in some
become a banner for lack of self-value on a poor Black woman.

As a people, Black Americans have been pleading for health-care facilities and state officials alike to value and see our families as worthy. Black Americans are the "other," sequestered away in unwanted physician training facilities to be cared for by rugged fair-skinned cowboys desperate to show their bootstraps. We are different enough to be seen in unwanted facilities by unwanted practitioners that don't admire us but similar enough to require a traditional burial when we meet our demise. The expansion of COVID, the new Spanish flu, has exacerbated an already defective health-care environment. I am personally left straddled between two worlds, one that is treacherously run by those that have always had the upper hand, and one that is more natural but void of power. Johanna has taught me that this path has been taken before, living in two worlds. *Take My Hand, Precious Lord.*

The new pandemic has taught me that the fears of our community are as real and ever present as the cacti in the cemetery. The sharp spike protein capsule of the virus brings sharp pain and fear that echo the sting from the cactus needle. When the horror of COVID is burned away, I am left with the soft undertones of a reminder that our perseverance and love for our community is sweet and nourishing but never admired by the cowboy riding into the sunset. This isn't the first time our perseverance has gone unnoted. The same snarling monster of racism that filled so many graves prematurely is just as alive today as it was in 1918. At the beginning of the current medical pandemic, the intersection of the long-lasting pandemic, racism, was met. We were left with the idea of feeling a classic trope, donning a bandanna for safety given the lack of a face mask. Although we have no spikes to pierce and inflict pain, we are feared more than the cacti and the virus. Black bodies overfilling the morgues are renderings of forgotten last breaths whispered away in cold, sterile hospitals; Black bodies are the moniker of limited supplies, invisible social lines, and separation chronically present in our communities created by a line drawn in the sand by those that always saw us as "other." *Take my Hand, precious Lord, and lead me home.*

The cacti in the cemetery became my training ground for navigating COVID, a reminder that I am not the first poor Black woman to cross this path, nor the last. I am pushed to lean on lessons that tombstones have taught me about perseverance and faith. Over the past few years, COVID has become the ever-present terror ready to cause lightning nerve pain at the slightest touch. The lessons learned from the tombstones became my only mode of survival during the pandemic and my place to rest spiritually. My profession in health care pushed me long ago to confront my own mortality. COVID has caused me to examine my possible reality; if I am to die, I will become a part of the field of tombstones. I will be a tombstone for others to lean on when needed, providing guidance and hope. My life's value does not come from the academic degrees I have acquired or things I have purchased; my value comes from what I leave future generations. *When my way grows dreary, precious Lord, lead me near.*

I want to live in a narrative of peaceful oak trees and calm still nights, a place where health care is an equalizer and a marvelous savior. However, I was raised on a battleground of reality concreted over with hate. A picturesque narrative of rolling hills transitions into one of blood-tinged soil and weakened concrete that softly whispers encouraging words for me to soldier on, keep moving forward. I will be ever spiritually present among the tombstones until we are nourished by justice. I know that I will lead and be led forward just as were those who came before me. *Take my hand, precious Lord, and lead me home.*

References

Jackson, Mahalia. 1956. "Take My Hand, Precious Lord." Lyrics by Thomas A. Dorsey. *Bless This House.* Columbia Records, CL 899. Vinyl.

CHAPTER 3

A Mother's Healing

Afro-Caribbean Women, Ancestral Healing Knowledge, and a Global Pandemic

Sara Jean-Francois

Day 1: Headache . . . I brush it off, take ibuprofen, drink coffee, and run out the door.

Day 2: Headache . . . "OK, maybe it will go away."

Day 3: Headache . . . "Hey, I don't think I can come into work today."

Day 4: Sleep . . .

Day 5: My eyes hurt so bad I can't stand to open them, I can't eat, my throat aches . . . sleep

Day 6: Call my mom . . .

Day 7: I don't even know. . . .

.

.

.

Day 10: I get tested . . .

When I tested positive for COVID-19, I thought I had statistics on my side. I was young, I was healthy, I was employed, and I had good health insurance! And honestly, this thing could not be as bad as they say. We know the symptoms, go about our days with caution, and wash our hands every chance we get. But when I got sick, I worried less about how I got it and more about how I would beat it. For me, it was never about having access to health care, although I do not take this privilege lightly; it was about being away from my mother and being too prideful to admit I needed her.

Day 1 was my very first day living in my newly rented apartment. Although I lived close to my mother, my move out of her house along with the huge disagreement that led to our present situation did not leave much room for me to go running back to mommy. So, for the first three days, I said nothing about what I was feeling, and I overlooked the fact that my symptoms seriously aligned with what the CDC said to look out for. That was a mistake on my part. After days of a pounding headache, with me unable to open my eyes or eat, my mom came to get me at my apartment and insisted I stay at her house until I was feeling better.

The day the doctors called me to tell me I tested positive for COVID, the rest of the world was only a week into what would become several months of lockdown in Massachusetts and countless other states and countries. I was sleeping in my old bed at my mom's house when I got the call; the doctors advised me to go back to my apartment because I lived alone, and this way, I could self-isolate. My symptoms appeared manageable, so I insisted on going home. Of course, my mother said it was a bad idea, but I just brushed it off and said, "it's doctor's orders." But, leave it to my Haitian mother to prove these doctors wrong because not three days later, my mother was rushing to my apartment and taking me to the hospital. She decided then and there that I was packing a bag and staying with her until my test came back negative! One thing about my mom: ain't nobody telling her no or that she's wrong. So I didn't argue.

For weeks, I sat alone, quarantined, afraid of infecting those around me, and wondering how it happened. How did I get this? What did I do wrong? And most importantly, I said to myself, no one can find out! So, as I rewatched *Sex and the City* and binged old Black love movies online, I also hid from social media and only told my closest friends. Although this seclusion didn't matter much: before my test results had reached me, my mother had managed to recite a complete medical diagnostic through landline! Hitting all the major Haitian hubs—New York, Haiti, and, of course, Florida. News of my sickness had gone international! By the time I had risen from my afternoon nap, I had dozens of missed calls, text messages, and WhatsApp video requests! And so, my journey to recovery began.

Thinking of my experience with this virus, I felt it was important not only to reflect on the very long six weeks I spent in my old room in my mother's home, alone, but also to document how crippling it can feel having to be nursed when for so long you had been able to stand on your own. Most importantly, however, my story is only made possible because of the ancestral healing knowledge my mother was able to obtain through this international landline and centuries of Haitian remedies.

We all know that the treatment of Black women in our health-care system has been and remains deplorable, whether this is in the maternity wards where Black women are six times more likely to suffer from birth complications in comparison to their white counterparts (Bridges 2011), or in the primary care offices where Black women are sent home with Tylenol while their white counterparts are given prescriptions for stronger pain relief. In a 2019 opinion piece titled "More People Are Talking About Black Women's Periods—and That's a Good Thing," Ashley Simpo discusses the increasing public discourse surrounding Black women's health and wellness. The ugly truth is that doctors do not hear us because of the anti-Black racism that inhibits basic patient care for Black women. Simpo writes, "Our health is in the hands of doctors who do not hear us when we say we're in pain." This is exactly how I felt when doctors asked me blanket statements about pain but never actually listened for my response. From birth control experimentation in Puerto Rico to the forced sterilization of

Black women during the eugenics movement, cases of medical misconduct have led to widespread mistrust of medical professionals for numerous Black people throughout the United States. More recently, in April 2020, two French researchers who were invited onto a French TV network to discuss the lasting effects of COVID-19 proposed that COVID-19 vaccines be tested on African people (Rosman 2020). This modern-day representation of anti-Blackness in medical research and health care shows that the mistrust of the medical community, physicians, and researchers held by many Black people is not unfounded. This mistrust has made room for the ongoing development of many traditional remedies from non-Western cultures, including the Haitian culture.

But even knowing all of this, I remain amazed at how indifferent hospital staff and doctors were when it came to my health. In the six weeks that I was sick, I discussed my symptoms—which evolved from a headache to a high fever, to loss of appetite, smell, and taste— with several health-care professionals. I was repeatedly given only one piece of advice. "Take Tylenol." Even as I explained that these headaches would result in blurry vision and the inability to open my eyes or even so much as see a hint of light, doctors insisted that Tylenol would do the trick.

"Doctor, I have a sore throat!" Tylenol.

"Doctor, my fever is getting worse!" Tylenol.

"Doctor, I've had this terrible headache for two days now!" Tylenol.

"Doctor, my body really aches!" Tylenol.

"Doctor, you remember that headache I told you about? I've had it for four days now, and it won't go away!" Tylenol.

The very reason I continued to go to work, aside from it being my primary source of income, is because all my life, doctors have written off my concerns as trivialities or just paranoia. For that reason, I didn't second-guess a headache or fatigue even as our country was on the cusp of a pandemic. My experience is not unlike that of thousands of Black women in the United States. As a means of combating the ongoing dismissal of our health concerns, our cultures have created and crafted methods of preventative medicine. I grew up trying all the Haitian remedies, then as a last resort going to the hospital. Sure, I would do my annual checkups, but I quickly learned how to self-manage and not disclose it to my primary care physicians if I did have a concern. When I realized I was constantly getting motion sickness, my mother prescribed a pot of cloves, garlic leaves, and hot water. My mother prescribed peppermint tea, ibuprofen, and a hot towel when my periods got so bad that I couldn't go to school. She has never led me astray. So, when I contracted COVID, and my mother (fully gowned, gloved, and double-masked) came into the room I was staying in with some hot chocolate–looking beverage and said "drink," I sure did—even while gagging the whole time.

My mother is not a doctor, simply a health-care worker with twenty-five years of experience and a legacy of traditional remedies to support her decisions. But she did get it right with COVID, just like she had gotten it right countless times before. Traditional remedies are not usually about attacking one symptom. The remedies are not like an antiviral or an antibiotic, but rather like a preventative measure. These remedies are not about a cure. They are about giving the whole body the energy and ingredients it needs to heal itself. When I initially became ill, my mother's first observation was my fever. All my life, she instructed me to use hot oils like Haitian castor oil, *lwil maskriti*, and layer up when fighting any sickness; this virus was no different. When I came home, the first thing she did was roll up her sleeves and pull out the oil. It took a couple of days, but when my fever did break, believe me, it felt like emerging out of clouds, and for the first time in nearly a month my head was clear.

Fever aside, another big obstacle we faced was how effectively this virus attacked every part of my body. The fatigue, muscle weakness, and shortness of breath proved to be the most difficult to get past. For this, my mother prescribed tea. But not just any old tea bag, teas rich in antioxidants so that the toxic and damaging organisms in your body—the virus—can't live inside. My mother figured this out more quickly than most, and I think this was the key to my recovery. She used traditional Haitian remedies throughout my experience with COVID, but one tea in particular made a world of difference. Mixing cloves, crushed garlic, cinnamon, and salt created a rich tea filled with antioxidants, effectively cleaning out my system. I had to drink this three times a day in addition to that hot chocolate–looking beverage I mentioned earlier. I later learned this was called *punch*; she blended aloe, rum, eggs, evaporated milk, cinnamon, turmeric, and a little bit of ginger powder. This remedy is one made as a direct result of an emerging pandemic. It took telephone trees and a shared legacy of trial and error to create. I'm sure all the Caribbean WhatsApp chats were talking about "punch" when this pandemic hit.

Our mothers' connection to our culture and our traditional remedies have always kept us out of harm's way. This story I've told isn't as uncommon as I make it out to be. These remedies are most often a result of generations of Afro-Caribbean women looking for alternative medicine. It is a form of resistance; it is yet another way our resilient mothers refuse to let anyone take their babies away (see Barber 2017). For many, ancestral healing knowledge, or traditional cultural remedies, may seem nonscientific, or perhaps too obvious. Still, my culture and mother have taught me that our bodies are a healing force, and a powerful one at that. This pandemic has only brought to light how powerful generational knowledge, cultural remedies, and a mother's healing can really be.

References

Barber, Lauren. 2017. "Harriet's Squad: Black Women Using Ancient Healing Methods as Resistance." *Elle*, July 26, 2017. https://www.elle.com/culture/career-politics/a46954/harriets-apothecary-ancient-healing-resistance/.

Bridges, Khiara. 2011. *Reproducing Race: An Ethnography of Pregnancy as a Site of Racialization*. Berkeley: University of California Press.

Rosman, Rebecca. 2020. "Racism Row as French Doctors Suggest Virus Vaccine Test in Africa." *Al Jazeera*, April 4, 2020. https://www.aljazeera.com/news/2020/4/4/racism-row-as-french-doctors-suggest-virus-vaccine-test-in-africa.

Simpo, Ashley. 2019. "More People Are Talking About Black Women's Periods—and That's a Good Thing." *BET*, November 4, 2019. https://www.bet.com/article/tvn95s/op-ed-more-people-are-talking-about-black-women-s-periods.

CHAPTER 4

Sewing Healing

Research as Creative Ritual

Nimot Ogunfemi

From Where I'm Standing
Setting the Stage

We are currently in the thick of things of the novel coronavirus (COVID-19) pandemic. Now more than ever, the uncertain nature of the future is apparent. It is shrouded in mystery and lying in the dark. This reality is as anxiety provoking as it is inevitable. So how can we begin to reclaim and reimagine the dark? When I say reimagine, I do not mean making a new image but instead returning to an indigenous one. Reimagining in this sense is a process by which we remember what we have been conditioned to forget—that there is beauty, peace, and comfort in the dark.

From where I am standing, in early 2022, we are living in both tumultuous and inspiring times. The year 2020 proved to be unlike any other I have experienced. It was full of uncertainty, disappointment, triumph, and growth. More than a year after the ending of what many thought would be "the worst year ever," many pressing problems have yet to be resolved. I am (and we are) still amid a deadly pandemic, complicated by the unfortunately usual suspects. The environmental, race, class, and gender inequities that were not appropriately acknowledged before the pandemic continue to block its resolution. That is, our inability to address these concerns continues to inhibit our healthy development as a society. It stagnates us when we need (r)evolution the most. Our moment is relatively dark.

But of course, the last two years have not been *all* bad. The dark is more complicated than the simple "good" and "bad" dichotomy that plagues Western systems of knowledge. For me, the COVID-19 context has also proven to be an opportunity for immense personal growth and self-actualization. In this time, I came face-to-face with the -isms that threaten all of humanity. In months of solitude and isolation, I compassionately confronted myself. Like the 4.5 million Americans who quit their jobs in November 2021 alone (U.S. Bureau of Labor Statistics 2022), I recognized the opportunity to bravely swim against the current of capitalist work culture despite the push to go with its flow. While many felt a great longing to "go back to normal," I realized I had never been given a chance to define what *my* normal is. One responsibility of liberation is self-determination and self-definition. For me, this important work took place in the dark. This space of uncertainty proved to be challenging, inspirational, and transformative. As I let go of the need to control, the first flowers of healing began to bloom here.

A Black transnational feminist positionality allowed me to embrace and critique the global moment, encouraged me to wander freely in transformative spiritual spaces, and facilitated the study of my soul. In this chapter, I explore the process and outcomes of a disciplined self-research practice that I call a *ritual of research*. Through this ritual of research, I exhibit my newfound affinity for the dark, home in on spiritual power, and engage in a liberatory creative practice. One outcome of my autoethnographic journey is a self-portrait titled *Sewing Healing* (figure 4.1) which was displayed at the University of Illinois Krannert Art Museum as part of Dr. Blair Smith's exhibition titled *Homemade, with Love* (2020–21).

In this work, I am most influenced by transnational Black feminism, which is built on two basic assumptions: (1) working across borders and cultures is an essential feature of our contemporary world, and (2) specific locations and identities must be the basis of any analysis (Davies 2014). My Black transnational feminism is Pan-African

FIGURE 4.1 Nimot Ogunfemi, *Sewing Healing*, mixed-media collage, 2020.

in that I am interested in the connectedness, merits, and well-being of African-descendant people all over the world. African feminist approaches to healing include an aim to utilize indigenous philosophies and traditional problem-solving. Black feminist approaches to healing often endorse art as a tool for critical consciousness and well-being.

I am deeply invested in and inspired by the physical, spiritual, and political healing work that has been done throughout the Diaspora for centuries. One group doing such work is the Women of Irmandande da Boa Morte (Sisterhood of the Good Death), the oldest organization of African-descendant womxn in the Americas, founded in Brazil by enslaved Fon and Ewe womxn (James 2018). They, too, honor the ancestors and their legacies of Black liberation. These and other transnational Black women represent rich knowledge bases, to which I refer in times of change or uncertainty.

My individual (and collective) processes of reimagining have taught me that darkness can be transformative in its ability to pinpoint my anxieties and facilitate the confrontation of my fears. Surrounded by the darkness of a new era, I wondered what it would be like to enter the dark without running to the light for safety. I wanted to remain submerged there, not drowning or sinking in darkness but floating. I wondered whether I could somehow emerge with new knowledges (Troutman and Johnson 2018) and a willingness to share this knowledge.

As it turns out, I both could and did. When I was feeling sedentary at home, I began a practice of Kemetic yoga, facilitated by YouTubers like Sarah Wes (then located in Egypt) and the teachings of Black women yoginis in the community like my former Vinyasa instructor Destinee. When I felt most isolated, I listened deeply to the birds singing outside my window. I wished to communicate with them to show my gratitude for their company. I somehow found my own ways to thank them. I processed using an arts-based practice when I was overwhelmed with emotion (which is common these days). This included journaling, collaging, and sound editing my way through the emotion. When I was advised to seek safety, I had to answer hard questions about where I really felt safe and at home. Before I could travel to Tanzania physically, I did so spiritually. Following my heart and listening to my soul led me right back to the continent. *Sewing Healing* is the visual representation of these practices and the product of my ritual of research. In all these mundanely sacred practices, I engaged in something that felt deeply natural, indigenous even.

Starting with Self

But I cannot act as if these realizations around my healing practices were serendipitous. No, they are a culmination of my identities and the experiences that affirm or challenge them. My preference for the indigenous is deeply encoded in my blood, which holds the shared memories and experiences of hundreds of ancestors. My last name (Ogunfemi) connects me to the Yoruba people of Nigeria and their indigenous religion. I learned the value of heritage and a love of land and country from my fraternal family. My maternal family taught me about Black power and soul, resistance, and respect for the sacrifices of my ancestors. I am a child of the Diaspora. Africa is rooted in my heart and is usually at the forefront of my mind.

I am a healer (of self and community). I am in my last stages of a doctoral degree in counseling psychology at the University of Illinois under the mentorship of liberation psychologist Dr. Helen Neville. While I am proud of my academic achievements, I do not believe my path to healing began with me. More accurately, I found a place in a legacy of healers. I am the daughter of a healer (occupational therapist) born and raised on the South Side of Chicago and the great-great-granddaughter of a healer (herbalist) from Abeokuta, Nigeria. From my upbringing, I learned how to take care of family and community using spoken medicine, herbal healing, and spiritual care.

Much of what I know about healing has been passed on to me by Black women. This means I know well the merits of our methods. I understand the specific concerns that weigh heavy on a Black woman's heart. I find my role in the feminist movement here. I want to be where women (and men) need to regenerate their spirits from the violence of patriarchy. My Black feminist healer identity also demands that I prioritize prevention. My work isn't just about responding to psychospiritual pain but about doing what I can to help others avoid it.

To be a healer is to be a student of people, constantly learning from them and about them. I started at our collective source in my quest to heal Black people. My most formative learning occurred both outside of the classroom and outside of the United States. Africa is my most influential community learning space. I visited Lagos, Nigeria, for the first time at sixteen years old. Much to my family's surprise, I loved the hustle of the city and its frequent power outages. They were my first lessons in the beauty and transformative power of darkness. I returned to the continent again at twenty-four, this time to the East Coast. Experiences in Tanzania have changed my idea of what it means to do good and relevant research. Observing and interacting with the land helped me reemphasize a connection to nature. Conversations with traditional healers (*waganga* in Swahili) gave me firsthand experiences with indigenous wellness practices. My study of the Swahili language has led me to many culturally rich spaces, sharing ideas with some of the country's most brilliant citizens. As with Ghana for Cynthia B. Dillard (2008), Tanzania has played a big role in my intellectual and spiritual position.

Exploring my intersectionality helped me make sense of these multicultural identities and the responsibilities associated with them. Before COVID-19, I had begun more explicit explorations and integrations of my identities as a researcher and an artist, but the circumstances surrounding the pandemic gave that process a major boost. Like many in my community, I can find inspiration in different emotional and physical spaces. But something about seeing people fighting over toilet paper, hoarding groceries, and weaponizing (metaphorically and literally) the spread of the disease amid the threat of national economic crisis just heightened my ability. I became increasingly interested in creative ways to maintain my wellness. Beyond that, I wanted to share that rich information that oppressive education systems marginalize.

Science and Spirit

One fallacy of the Western patriarchal education system is the presumed polarity of science and spirituality. This assumption would lead one to believe the two cannot coexist. But science and spirit are more proximal than polar. To facilitate indigenous African feminist research, Bagele Chilisia and Gabo Ntseane (2010) used indigenous rituals during focus groups with Botswanan women. I often illustrate the compatibility of science and spirit with my research as well. My dissertation is centered on the everyday practices of care and traditional spiritual healing among Tanzanians. In this and other projects, I attempt to scientifically capture the spirit. My African worldview, sharpened with transnational Black feminist thought, makes the compatibility of science and spirituality crystal clear. I acknowledge the continuity between science and spirit to honor my multicultural identities and engage in authentic research.

As one can imagine, my spiritually scientific position is incompatible with the majority of research paradigms and methods. One methodology that does allow me to practice spiritual research is autoethnography. This methodology offers many opportunities to explore the borderlands between science and spirit. Emerging in the 1970s, autoethnography is a research approach that aims to analyze personal experience to make meaning of cultural experiences (Ellis 2004). Many Black feminist researchers have used this approach to similarly examine their own spirit/soul (Dillard and Bell, 2011; Griffin 2012; Norwood 2018). My specific approach to autoethnography is arts based. Arts-based autoethnography offers the opportunity to transcend the limitations of written and oral language by using art to make meaning. When used intentionally, this hybrid methodology can also be healing to the mind, body, and soul.

Ritual(s) of Research

Just as most research in counseling psychology aims to illuminate and improve the condition of the soul, rituals of research play a supportive role. Research's long-term relationship with ritual did not begin with autoethnography. Ritual has in many ways always been a part of qualitative research approaches. The mandatory thirty to forty-five minutes reserved for processing after every interview, the reading of informed consent that ensures ethical practices, and even the interview itself with a loose (or tight) set of questions can all be considered rituals of research. My articulation of ritual of research reaches beyond seventeenth-century science into the more ancient practices and purposes of science. Working from here requires an academic awakening, a remembrance of the indigenous uses of science. Sobonfu Somé (2000, 43–44) writes: "In the West, people tend to standardize everything, so if you describe one ritual, people think it applies to all situations. Even though every case is different, people will follow the same formula. In ritual, that doesn't work. A ritual has to be made specific to the people who are involved in it. And if you try to standardize things, you actually take away the spirit of the person and try to force something false into the situation." Here, she touches on what many Black womxn are confronted with in academia, the presumptuous tendency toward knowledge based in standardization. My ritual is highly individualized, based on my cultural heritage, emotional expression, and intellectual background.

As Somé reminds us, the essence of ritual and the science behind its success is personalization. This contradicts the standardization that modern science prides itself on. This tension between generalization and individual utility is eased by indigenous science. Similarly, I was not interested in taking away the individualized aspect of my research ritual. Stripping the science of its spirit would stop me from speaking directly to my soul and others'. In this project, I boldly tailored my ritual of research around my principles, needs, and aspirations. This is the kind of research I want to be a part of, and the type of project I love to cheer on from a distance.

What Is in a Ritual?

Ritual is a process that requires discipline, respect, and awareness. In ritual, we set an intention, make a sacred space, and invoke the divine (Somé 2004). Rituals are many things. They are steeped in tradition; the traditional aspect is evident whether practiced exactly as in ancient days or in radically new ways. Rituals are adaptive; they transcend space and time and have survived the harshest conditions. Rituals are repetitive; they happen periodically based on date or need. Rituals are educational; they teach us about ourselves, our community, the spiritual world. Through ritual, we make more sense of experience and process feelings. Most importantly, rituals are healing; they address some physical, spiritual, or general health needs. Rituals are not relegated to the religious. They are everywhere. Rituals are as mundane as getting your hair or nails done every two weeks and as sacred as jumping the broom.

Ritual is important to me because it is how I have come to know myself in relation to the interconnected world around me. Ritual helps me feel linked to the indigenous *livity* that calls out to me, even when I find myself in the most foreign situations. Ritual is the mold that holds together society, science, and spirituality. Traditionally, spiritual healers are influential members of society. My great-grandfather was counsel to a king in Abeokuta and valued for his ability to advise with and through the spirit. Throughout Africa, both men and women have played this respected role. For example, Alice Lakwena of Uganda was a military leader and spiritual healer who led a battalion of men against the government from 1986 to 1987 (Behrend 2000). Western scholars and their foreign variant of patriarchy have predictably focused on men as the heroes of healing. Their approach to knowledge silences the voice and contributions of womxn (Zungu et al. 2014). My approach to knowledge requires bearing witness to healing journeys facilitated by diverse Black women. Because I value our unique skills, competencies, and philosophies, I amplify my own and other Black women's experiences with healing. Additionally, other Black girls, womxn, and femmes can benefit from more homemade spaces of individual and community healing. We stand to gain much.

My Ritual of Research

In my arts-based autoethnographic project, I boldly tailored my ritual of research around my principles, needs, and aspirations. My discipled daily ritual of creatively responding to four processing questions facilitated a structured examination of myself and my spiritual healing/coping styles. Taking an unapologetically vested interest in my health and pursuing mental health knowledge led me on a scientifically motivated spiritual wellness journey.

Every day for three months, I journaled and collaged about the wellness of my soul. I responded to three questions (in no particular order) related to my spiritual well-being. First, I asked, *is all well with your soul?* Second, I asked, *what color and location do you associate with your spiritual well-being?* Finally, I asked, *with what image do you associate spiritual well-being?*

I responded to these three questions using critical incidents, poems, and quotes.[1] At times, I also responded using sound. While auditory data were not collected daily, they still informed the research process. I symbolized my day-to-day psychospiritual state with colored circles, later coded for meaning (using color), intensity (using size), and positionality (using location) (see figure 4.2). The multimodal approach stems from the need to capture the essence of my emotional

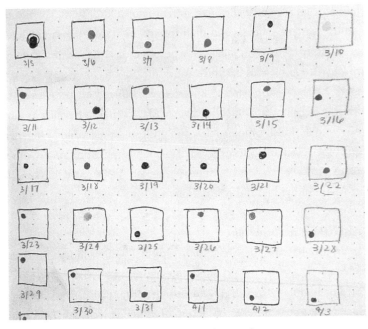

FIGURE 4.2 Responses to processing question no. 2.

experience. This required more than one tool of expression. Because the events, decisions, and future I contemplated felt very heavy, they had to be processed differently.

In *Uses of the Erotic: The Erotic as Power*, Audre Lorde (1978) confronts the spiritual/erotic and spiritual/political dichotomies. Similarly, my research ritual takes place in borderlands of the sacred and the mundane, in everyday, divine spaces, and in worldly meeting spaces of the spirit. These borderlands represent darkness for me because they aren't completely governed by any one dimension's laws of nature, like gravity and time (and thus have previously been avoided by many researchers). They are mysterious spaces (locations and states) that we come to know through individual and intertwined experiences with spirit. These spaces are both entirely available to some and unfathomable to others.

My studio apartment, a particularly mundane yet sacred space, was the setting for my ritual of research. Here at home, I invoked ancestors and elders that possess healing wisdom through my process of reflection and introspection. I believe that they can be called on during times of unrest, transition, or celebration. They respond to me in diverse ways, despite distances of time and space. For example, when I felt most lonely, I was spiritually directed to take in the sound of the birds outside my window. This reminded me that I am a part of a larger living and nonliving community, thus never *really* alone.

My ritual was shrouded in tradition and included many indigenous practices, images, and symbols. As the days of working from home increased, so did my urge to wear traditional clothes. With little need for business casual or other Western-designed dress codes, I found myself more frequently and comfortably wearing pieces of African wax fabric, called Ankara in Yoruba (or *kitenge* in Swahili), and kangas. A kanga is a piece of fabric, forty-five by sixty-five inches, mostly worn by Swahili womxn of East Africa. Kangas are multidimensional in that they communicate a host of social and interpersonal messages (called *ujumbe*), from flirting with a partner to suggesting dominance. A kanga's ujumbe, coupled with a woman's attitude, body language, and disposition, implicitly and explicitly communicates much.

Kangas are also multipurpose in that they can be used to carry babies, treated as blankets, given as a gift for a special occasion, or used to wish congratulations, good luck, blessings, or love. "Kanga, which embodies art, beauty, culture, and customs of coastal women, is almost mythical . . . and there is more to it than meets the eye" (Hamid 1996, 103). As such, the kanga is several things. It is the word-limited social media post that predates the Internet. It is a soft-spoken but loud womxn, wrapped in vibrantly designed fabrics, with short and clever proverbs, messages, prayers, slogans, and affirmations. It is as if someone told Swahili womxn centuries ago to "do Twitter *but make it fashion."* It is womxn saying everything they want to say, without saying anything at all. The kanga can also be explicitly political. On kanga as a political strategy, Saida Yahya-Othman (1997, 135) writes: "In Tanzania, the kanga indexes this 'femininity' in a strong way. . . . The messages that appear on the kanga are viewed as a uniquely female form of communication, and women in Zanzibar . . . have been making increasing use of them as an additional strategy that allows them to make strong statements about their concerns while at the same time avoiding any direct conflict which may arise from their individual actions."

The communicative nature of the kanga is reminiscent of how Black womxn in America used the quilt to weave messages and maps of physical freedom and spiritual liberation (Rosa and Orey 2009). The viewer of *Sewing Healing* can see dancing multicolored dots sewn onto the canvas in a gridlike fashion throughout the kanga at the foreground (see figure 4.3). These dots represent the responses to my second question; they are the colors I associated with my spiritual well-being. I chose color because it can be used to explain both common associations (e.g., "yellow, because it was a sunny day and I felt happy") and more complex and abstract ideas (e.g., "maroon, because it is red, which I associate with anxiety, and some black, which I associate with mystery or uncertainty"). This combinatory approach to color and emotion allows for the descriptive accuracy of feelings that are often complex and not experienced in isolation. The emotional road map aspect of the piece and the sewing method also directly reference the quilt making of the nineteenth and twentieth centuries.

Specifically, my inclination to sew the circles found throughout the kanga onto the canvas, weaving the colorful and kinetic story of my spiritual well-being into the artwork, was informed by African American womxn's quilting. On the tradition of quilting, Darlene Clark Hine (1982, 361) writes:

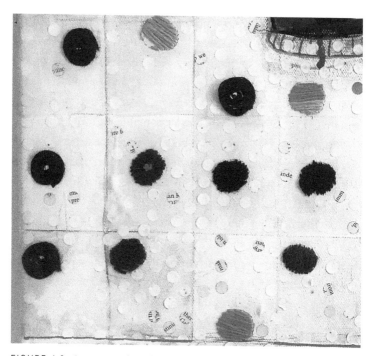

FIGURE 4.3 *Sewing Healing*, kanga ujumbe detail.

African-American women, as slaves and freedwomen, could convert the utilitarian quilt into an object of art and transform quilting into a social and cultural community affair.... It is especially suggestive that quilting became a creative process whereby unschooled, rural, southern black women could give voice and vision, structure and substance, to their personal and spiritual lives. On a related note, a contemporary black woman artist, Samella Lewis, reminds us that African art rose above its roots in utility, indeed that the majority of works of African art were made to fulfill the needs of the communities.

As used by Black womxn, the quilt was accessible, political, and relational. For this ritual of research, I sewed the dots onto the kanga. I wanted this creative practice to similarly enact liberation and artistic

voice while simultaneously honoring the creative connections between African womxn and African American womxn. Like the kanga,
the quilt has both style and function. Like the quilt and the kanga, my
work's hidden yet present message is of the utmost importance. The
beauty and utility of kanga inspired me to think about creative ways I
can invoke the power of this East African fiber art form.

My ritual was intentional. I began to contemplate speaking healing over the people most directly descended from Africa in a similar
fashion. As intention is key to my ritual of research, I would now like
to state mine. I realized early in this process that I was creating for the
sake of individual and group survival by engaging in individualized
culturally informed healing. I approached self-research as a process
of moving inward toward introspection and simultaneously outward
toward spiritual connection. With this particular ritual of research,
I wanted to align my personal and academic values, think critically
about the sociopolitical moment, and make meaning of unexpected
circumstances. Strengthening my skills in such work gives me multidimensional artillery against capitalist patriarchal and colonialist
systems of science.

My kanga's ujumbe in *Sewing Healing* reads: KWENYE UPWEKE
HAUKO PEKE YAKO, PONA KWENYE UPWEKE WAKO, which translates to "*Even in isolation, you are not alone, heal in your solitude*"
(see figure 4.4). This form of writing, reading, and talking reaches
for healing. It directly responds to the ongoing intellectual, medical,
and spiritual injustices against Black people. The piece accesses the
traditional African healing tool of *spoken medicine* to enact healing.

My ritual was healing. The figure in the portrait is, in part, mine.
Painting myself as the subject helped me feel more empowered than
marginalized. Around the fourth week of documentation, I started to
feel the physical effects of having limited mobility and being home-
bound. In response, I began a practice of Kemetic yoga via YouTube.
Often wrapped in a kanga or kitenge for this practice, I could recon-

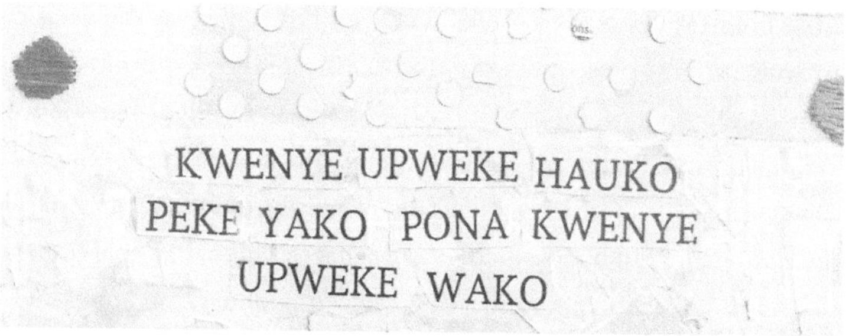

KWENYE UPWEKE HAUKO
PEKE YAKO PONA KWENYE
UPWEKE WAKO

FIGURE 4.4 *Sewing Healing*, text detail from kanga ujumbe.

nect with myself physically and learn more about indigenous Egyptian philosophy and religion. This gave me a sense of wisdom and ethical grounding. In *Sewing Healing* I am doing a variation of the pose of Anpu, one arm raised in the air. While in this pose, I felt confident and as if I was pledging allegiance to Africa, its ways, and its wisdom. When I was physically distanced from the continent with no sure hope of returning any time soon, this was comforting to me. Processing and naming my feelings every day helped me feel in control of them, not controlled by them. Below the kanga in *Sewing Healing*, there are three pairs of collaged legs dressed in indigenous jewelry and body paint. This is a visual affirmation of what the kanga reads. Through these figures, I wanted to invoke the spirit of indigenous knowledge and the connectedness of global Black communities.

Women's Work

This work is in conversation with several Black womxn artists and scholars. Fine artists Billie Zangewa and Faith Ringgold, who work with themes of domesticity and storytelling, are major inspirations for this project. Like them, I wanted to explore how I create and define my own domestic space. Ringgold's *Change 3* (1991) and *Marlon Riggs: Tongues Untied* (1994) centralize a story-like portrait and use aspects of traditional African American quilting, with pieced fabric incorporated alongside acrylic on canvas. For Ringgold, the decision to work in fabric was personal and political, and it did not go unpunished by her white counterparts. She later recalled that she was sidelined for doing what was considered "women's work" (Ringgold 2012). Zangewa's *Cold Shower* (2019), *High Hopes* (2019), and *In My Solitude* (2018), all hand-stitched silk collages, show scenes of domesticity and satisfactory solitude. In these works, she wanted to use fabric because: "This thing we all have a daily relationship with is often dismissed by the world as mundane and unimportant, much like the daily, mundane work that women do to keep a home, a community, and a society going. I wanted to use this dismissed cultural thing to speak against patriarchy by creating powerful images about the importance of another dismissed thing, domesticity and the ordinary but important aspects of women's daily life and work in and around the home" (Okoro 2020). In my work, I was interested in my domestic space and moment. I explored how I had already prepared for this moment by filling my modest studio with enough and particular books, artwork, family photos, seasonings, comfy socks, and kangas to keep me satisfied and inspired.

My process was also a part of a larger legacy in the overlaps of research and community healing. African womxn on the continent and in the Diaspora have done much work to decolonize the research setting through methodologies congruent with indigenous African practices, like art making. Bagele Chilisa and Gabo Ntseane (2010) explain that decolonizing research helps envision other ways of theorizing complexities and understanding that recognize the connection between African and Western feminisms and build relationships grounded in ethicality and transformative respect and healing. I received much wisdom from Cynthia B. Dillard's (2008) endarkened feminist epistemology, which honors the wisdom, spirituality, and interventions of the ways the Black transnational womxn have come to know both inside and outside of research spaces.

A Spiritual Labor of Love and Its Fruit

My ritual of research had both artistic and spiritual outcomes. *Sewing Healing* is a mixed-media self-portrait that uses collage, paint, and text. Central to this autoethnographic self-portrait is the kanga turned emotional road map. It covers the figure just as I used to cover myself during isolation. Additionally, after the research, I was able to declare that *when physically distanced from Africa, I can heal from ongoing pain through a research ritual of experience, interpretation, and creation with the mere knowledge I have of the continent.* Through this research ritual, I began healing from racial and gender injustice and the anxiety that often accompanies uncertainty. I began to heal from a physical distance from Africa in several ways. I processed my current circumstances. This daily practice of creative processing enabled me to make sense of and meaning of the moment. While distanced from Africa physically, I used knowledge and memories from Africa as spiritual medicine.

Next, I incorporated an indigenous identity and tradition of knowing into a Western context. This helped me realize the compatibility of my multicultural and researcher identities. I left with practice with a renewed sense of self-efficacy as a spiritual being. In naming my feelings, I reclaimed a sense of self-determination and self-articulation. During a time of great confusion, I found clarity in my African culture. This proved liberatory when the dangers of capitalism and patriarchy were quite evident. I also gained a heightened sense of connectedness with the natural world around me, including the spirits living there. The birds, trees, and sun all took on new significance for me at that time. The most valuable outcome from my ritual of research was my notably enhanced spiritual well-being.

This work has much significance. My student status and physical location in America necessitate some degree of integration of ideas to meet national professional and academic standards. What makes my institutional education experiences more relevant is the active recognition of my African and feminine identities. This responsibly facilitates my personal/professional development. It promotes an authenticity that makes me feel a sense of congruence and belonging, despite explicit and implicit behaviors from the institution that may suggest otherwise. It was also healing for me to think creatively and critically about my community and my status as *never alone*. Finally, not being limited to one language or form of expression was healing. Of particular importance was utilizing a language of Bantu origin (Swahili). Black communities traditionally recognize the value in the arts as expression and knowledge production. I stand in agreement with that through my utilization of the fine arts, history, and psychology in this ritual of research.

Another outcome of this project was a research practice focused on creativity. This worked to decolonize the research process, highlight the wisdom and power of the indigenous, ignite the radical imagination, and make space for radical care (Chigudu 2015; Lewis 2007). Through this, I not only embrace the dark but use it as facilitative of individual and collective power and healing. It stands as testament to the space the virus has given us to implement ritual and the opportunity to embrace the darkness. This approach to research is liberation focused.

Despite its ability to heal and transform, this work is not easy. Some challenges to African indigenous rituals of research can include cultural imperialism, white supremacy, patriarchal approaches to education, Cartesian dualism, and professional pressure. In academia, there exists a tendency to pathologize Black spiritual realities. These are the hurdles that indigenous and other Black feminist scholars need to not only clear but demolish. On the other side of these hurdles are healing, self-actualization, and community empowerment. For centuries, white men have nurtured an academic culture that amplifies their realities and supports their interests. Their unquestioned ability to practice authentic science has inflated their confidence to the point of arrogance. It's high time for a change. Here, in this calling for a shift, one can hear the demand for social justice. Whether or not the global white minority responds to that call, there is still work to be done by the feminists of the Black and brown global majority. What we stand to gain is immeasurable.

Conclusion

For me, the dark has proven to be a space of spiritual reconnection and true authenticity. It is the space that allows for the most accurate self/soul reflection and where most of the following project occurs. During my ritual of research, I began to think about the work that can only be done in the darkness and the parts of me that are only revealed there too. When we fear and demonize the dark, we become preoccupied with the version of ourselves that others can see. We miss important opportunities to explore essential aspects of the self, nurture fear, and avoid the realities of our natural novice.[2]

In the darkness, I can be myself as a spiritual scientist. I can confront fears that slow me down and access the spirit creatively. Equipped with a love for indigenous science and spirituality, I bravely faced inevitable complexities to find moments of healing when peace of mind seemed distant. Only when swallowed by warm darkness and submerged without illumination, could I use my arts-based researcher identity to sew healing. I invite other Black femmes, girls, and womxn to engage in the similarly authentic and healing work that will save not only themselves but their communities as well.

Through a daily creative practice that included journaling, collage making, and sound, I embarked on a scientific journey of spiritual well-being. I used indigenous spiritual wisdom to access art-based rituals of research as healing in a time of mass isolation and global anxiety. My scientific self-portrait is a prayer, affirmation, emotional road map, and manifestation. I have read its text out loud countless times in moments of fear, isolation, or doubt. I documented my research to encourage the reader/viewer to read aloud or in spirit with me. In doing so, they stand in agreement and manifest collaboratively. In the company of the birds, the wind, the sun, the cicadas, the trees, I am (and we are) never alone. In the virtual company of others, ancestors, spirit, and self, I am (and we are) never alone. May this knowledge continue to carry us through the unforeseen future, *Aṣe.*

Notes

1.   A critical incident is a significant experience that has affected or influ-
     enced a specific person or people. It is an important turning point or time
     of personal change and is often used in narrative forms of data collection.
2.   Natural novice here is a reference to the existential theory of psychother-
     apy. In this school of thought, all humans (including the therapist and the
     client) dismantle unequal power dynamics. Rollo May and Irvin D. Yalom
     (1989) suggested that both parties are "fellow travelers" on a journey of
     life. In this journey, we acquire and share knowledge. We rarely, if ever,
     truly "master" life because we are constantly learning.

References

Behrend, Heike. 2000. *Alice Lakwena & the Holy Spirits: War in Northern Uganda, 1975–97.* Athens: Ohio University Press.

Chigudu, Daniel. 2015. "Assessing Policy Initiatives on Traditional Leadership to Promote Electoral Democracy in Southern Africa." *Mediterranean Journal of Social Sciences* 6 (1 S1): 120–26.

Chilisa, Bagele, and Gabo Ntseane. 2010. "Resisting Dominant Discourses: Implications of Indigenous, African Feminist Theory and Methods for Gender and Education Research." *Gender and Education* 22 (6): 617–32.

Davies, Carole Boyce. 2014. "Pan-Africanism, Transnational Black Feminism and the Limits of Culturalist Analyses in African Gender Discourses." *Feminist Africa* 19: 78–93.

Dillard, Cynthia B. 2008. "When the Ground Is Black, the Ground Is Fertile: Exploring Endarkened Feminist Epistemology and Healing Methodologies in the Spirit." In *Handbook of Critical and Indigenous Methodologies,* edited by Norman K. Denzin, Yvonna S. Lincoln, and Linda Tuhiwai Smith, 277–92. Thousand Oaks, Calif.: Sage.

Dillard, Cynthia B., and Charlotte Bell. 2011. "Endarkened Feminism and Sacred Praxis: Troubling (Auto) Ethnography Through Critical Engagements with African Indigenous Knowledges." *Counterpoints* 379: 337–49.

Ellis, Carolyn. 2004. *The Ethnographic I: A Methodological Novel About Autoethnography*. Walnut Creek, Calif.: AltaMira Press.

Griffin, Rachel Alicia. 2012. "I AM an Angry Black Woman: Black Feminist Autoethnography, Voice, and Resistance." *Women's Studies in Communication* 35 (2): 138–57.

Hamid, Mahfoudha Alley. 1996. "Kanga: It Is More Than What Meets the Eye—A Medium of Communication." *African Journal of Political Science/ Revue Africaine de Science Politique* 1 (1): 103–9.

Hine, Darlene Clark. 1982. "To Be Gifted, Female, and Black." *Southwest Review* 67 (4): 357–69.

James, Susan. 2018. "Indigenous Epistemology Explored Through Yoruba Orisha Traditions in the African Diaspora." *Women and Therapy* 41 (1–2): 114–30.

Lewis, Desiree. 2007. "Feminism and the Radical Imagination." *Agenda: Empowering Women for Gender Equity* 21 (72): 18–31.

Lorde, Audre. 1978. *Uses of the Erotic: The Erotic as Power*. New York: Out and Out Books.

May, Rollo, and Irvin D. Yalom. 1989. "Existential Psychotherapy." In *Current Psychotherapies*, edited by Raymond J. Corsini and Danny Wedding, 363–402. Itasca, Ill.: F. E. Peacock.

Norwood, Carolette R. 2018. "Decolonizing My Hair, Unshackling My Curls: An Autoethnography on What Makes My Natural Hair Journey a Black Feminist Statement." *International Feminist Journal of Politics* 20 (1): 69–84.

Okoro, Enuma. 2020. "The Textile Artist Who's Always Known How to Care for Herself: Billie Zangewa on Strength, Femininity, and the Healing Nature of Domesticity." *Cut*, June 26, 2020. https://www.thecut.com/2020/06/artist -profile-billie-zangewa.html.

Ringgold, Faith. 2012. "Faith Ringgold: Artist and Activist." Uploaded May 16, 2012, by MAKERS. YouTube video, 3:30. https://www.youtube.com/watch ?v=Comf9SetjRA.

Rosa, Milton, and Daniel Clark Orey. 2009. "Symmetrical Freedom Quilts: The Ethnomathematics of Ways of Communication, Liberation, and Art." *Revista Latinoamericana de Etnomatemática* 2 (2): 52–75.

Somé, Sobonfu. 2000. *The Spirit of Intimacy: Ancient Teachings in the Ways of Relationships*. New York: HarperCollins.

Somé, Sobonfu. 2004. *Women's Wisdom from the Heart of Africa*. Boulder, Colo.: Sounds True, 2004.

Troutman, Stephanie, and Brenna Johnson. 2018. "Dark Water: Rememory, Bio-power, and Black Feminist Art." *Taboo: The Journal of Culture and Education* 17 (3): article 8. https://doi.org/10.31390/taboo.17.3.08.

U.S. Bureau of Labor Statistics. 2022. "Job Openings and Labor Turnover—November 2021." Released January 4, 2022. https://www.bls.gov/news.release/archives/jolts_01042022.pdf.

Yahya-Othman, Saida. 1997. "If the Cap Fits: Kanga Names and Women's Voice in Swahili Society." *Afrikanistische Arbeitspapiere: Schriftenreihe des Kölner Instituts für Afrikanistik* 51: 135–49.

Zungu, Mthunzi, Nozipho Manqele, Calda de Vries, Thato Molefe, and Muziwandile Hadebe. 2014. "HERstory: Writing Women into South African History." *Agenda: Empowering Women for Gender Equity* 28 (1): 7–17.

CHAPTER 5

Black Feminist Autoethnography

Centering Black Women's Experiences During the COVID-19 Pandemic

Kyrah K. Brown, J. Mercy Okaalet, Brandie Green,
Peace Ossom-Williamson, Maryam O. Funmilayo,
Kenyatta Dawson, Courtney Jackson,
Chizoba Uzoamaka Okoroma, and Tamaya Bailey

The histories of science, medicine, and healthcare are literally built on the bodies of Black women. How is it that our bodies have been instrumental in advances in these fields, when we still have some of the worse health outcomes in this country?

—Moya Bailey and Whitney Peoples, "Towards a Black Feminist Health Science Studies"

Despite the widespread availability of advanced health-care technologies built on Black women's bodies, we systematically experience disparate health and health-care outcomes due to persistent structural inequities (Gee and Ford 2011; Bailey et al. 2017). The onset of the COVID-19 pandemic has exacerbated existing inequalities that disproportionately affect Black women. On January 20, 2020, the first U.S. patient was diagnosed with COVID-19 (Harcourt et al. 2020). By January 2021, the United States had the highest number of COVID-19 cases and among the highest test-positive rates and COVID-19 population death rates in the world (Johns Hopkins Coronavirus Resource Center, n.d.). At the onset of the pandemic, public officials frequently touted the disease as the "great equalizer"

(Garza 2020; Mein 2020). In reality, COVID-19 has become the great magnifier of our country's underlying systems of oppression based on race, gender, and class (Louisias and Marrast 2020; Chandler et al. 2021; Connor et al. 2020; Reed 2020). The COVID-19 pandemic has disproportionately affected Black families, with Black people being 2.4 times more likely than white people to die from complications related to COVID-19 (Garg 2020). This racial disparity persists after adjusting for clinical risk and sociodemographic variables (e.g., age, income) (OpenSAFELY Collaborative et al. 2020; Office for National Statistics 2020). Black women are four to six times more likely to die from complications related to COVID-19 after adjusting for age and other sociodemographic characteristics (Office for National Statistics 2020; McDermott 2020). As is the case in other scientific literatures, Black women's voices are largely missing in the current scientific dialogues concerning COVID-19 prevention and treatment (Spates 2012; BMJ Gender Diversity Group 2020; Brown Speights et al. 2017; Chandler et al. 2021).

The purpose of this chapter is to recenter Black women's voices and experiences during the COVID-19 pandemic using Black feminist autoethnography. We first provide an overview of available research documenting the impacts of COVID-19 on Black women. Then, we share autoethnographic vignettes from five Black women from diverse backgrounds to illustrate their lived experiences during the COVID-19 pandemic. For these Black women, the autoethnographic vignette served as a tool to reflect on their personal triumphs and challenges and as means to resist the multiple forms of oppression that have intensified during the COVID-19 pandemic. This chapter contributes to the growing literature centered on Black women's lived experiences during the COVID-19 pandemic and, ultimately, informs COVID-19 prevention, research, and policymaking efforts that benefit Black women.

An Overview of the Impact of the COVID-19 Pandemic on Black Women in the United States

Black women living in the United States must encounter and navigate (unknowingly and knowingly) multiple forms of oppression based on race, gender identity, class, ability, sexual orientation, and so on that have been exacerbated by the COVID-19 pandemic (Chandler et al. 2021; Gee, Ro, and Rimoin 2020; Bowleg 2020). At the onset of the COVID-19 pandemic, inconsistent public health messaging about mask wearing and transmissibility was partly responsible for the COVID-19 infodemic—or increased spread of the disease due to the growing misinformation (Chandler et al. 2021; Schneider 2020; Laurencin and McClinton 2020). A significant consequence of ineffective health messaging and the initial lack of data disaggregation by race/ethnicity and gender was the Black immunity myth. The Black immunity myth occurred through implicit messaging, suggesting that Black people were not disproportionately affected by the virus (Laurencin and McClinton 2020; Jaiswal, LoSchiavo, and Perlman 2020). Grippingly, the Black immunity myth also arose during the height of the HIV pandemic—which continues to disproportionately affect Black women today (Jaiswal, LoSchiavo, and Perlman 2020). Furthermore, recent studies have reported high levels of confusion and uncertainty about COVID-19 information among Black women during the pandemic (Chandler et al. 2021), which has significant implications for disease prevention efforts.

The COVID-19 pandemic affects Black women regardless of socioeconomic position and occupation. Black women are most commonly employed in essential health-care, service, and education occupations, which have been associated with a heightened risk of COVID-19 infection (Gausman and Langer 2020; Baker, Peckham, and Seixas 2020; Frye 2020). A greater proportion of Black women also work in the restaurant, entertainment, travel, and transportation industries, which were most affected by public health mandates (e.g., facility shutdowns) that affect their financial security (Vavra 2020). Black women employed in professional or business services—professions that afford the ability to work remotely—do not necessarily experience greater relief. Considering that most informal family caregivers are women (Feinberg et al. 2011) and that there is a Black-white disparity in informal caregiving intensity (Cohen et al. 2019), Black women may experience more stress in the work-from-home environment (Connor et al. 2020).

The COVID-19 pandemic disproportionately affects Black women's health and health care. Black women report experiencing heightened levels of stress, depression, and anxiety during the COVID-19 pandemic (Gur et al. 2020; Jackson and Pederson 2020; Chandler et al. 2021). With the expectation of working full-time high-risk jobs, serving as caregivers within the home and their communities, and, in some cases, being the primary breadwinners, balancing these multiple roles efficiently comes at the cost of one's mental health. In terms of physical health, Black women already face higher rates of preventable chronic disease due to structural inequities caused by gendered racism (Gee and Ford 2011; Bailey et al. 2017). In consequence, these underlying chronic diseases ultimately put Black women at greater risk for COVID-19 morbidity and mortality (Gee, Ro, and Rimoin 2020; Stokes 2020). In the health-care system, there is a lost history of health-care professionals mistreating or refusing to believe Black women when they relay their concerns, conditions, and symptoms during clinical encounters (Chandler et al. 2021; Gee and Ford 2011; McLemore 2019; Chambers et al. 2021). This precedent has significant implications for COVID-19 testing and treatment among Black women.

Black women may face additional challenges, including food insecurity, lack of medical supplies, and, in some cases, gender-based violence or intimate partner violence due to lockdowns, curfews, and increased housing and work instability during the pandemic (Kofman and Garfin 2020; Anurudran et al. 2020; Chishlom 2020). The issue compounds for groups who experience further marginalization, such as Black transgender women, Black women with disabilities, and Black immigrant women. Black transgender women faced higher rates of violence before COVID-19, and they have higher rates of HIV, rate their health poorer than the general population, and face access and healthcare barriers due to discrimination and existing conditions (National Center for Transgender Equality 2020). Women with disabilities face additional anxieties around "crisis triage," in which they are deemed less worthy of saving during the pandemic (Armitage and Nellums 2020; Solomon, Wynia, and Gostin 2020). Also, some Black immigrant women are at increased risk of facing cultural and/or language barriers and thus limited access to health care or COVID-19 prevention efforts (Krug 2020; Gervasi 2020).

To date, only a few studies have exclusively focused on Black women's lived experiences during the COVID-19 pandemic (Louisias and Marrast 2020; Chandler et al. 2021; Lipscomb and Ashley 2020). The lived experiences and insights of Black women offer a "unique angle of vision" (Hill Collins 2009, 39) because of our unique positionalities within multiple systems of oppression. Black women have unique ways of knowing and understanding the world, which are yet to be fully disseminated (Davis 1999). Black women's voices and experiences can contribute to new knowledge that informs COVID-19 prevention, research, and policymaking. The following sections of this chapter describe Black feminist autoethnography and how it was used to illustrate Black women's lived experience during the COVID-19 pandemic.

A Black Feminist Autoethnography

Black feminist autoethnography is epistemologically grounded in Black feminist thought, which provides discourse for Black women's lived experiences (Griffin 2012; hooks 1989; Lorde 1984, 1988; Guy-

Sheftall 1995; Hill Collins 1996, 2009). Black feminism is rooted in the belief that "Black women are inherently valuable, that [Black women's] liberation is a necessity not as an adjunct to somebody else's but because of [Black women's] need as human persons for autonomy" (Taylor 2017, 18). As a methodology, Black feminist autoethnography is focused on the perspective and reflections of the author or researcher. It evolves through a reflexive process that incorporates creative writing, and transformation occurs through active engagement with the material (Chang 2008; Griffin 2012). It serves as a method by which Black women can "talk back" to the multiple systems of oppression (racism, sexism, ableism, classism, etc.) (Griffin 2012; Brown-Vincent 2019; hooks 1989). In the context of general public health literatures, there is an ongoing struggle to center Black women's voices so that they may speak "truth to power" and resist narratives that have been imposed on them or that simply represent them as numerical objects (Brown Speights et al. 2017; Doll, Hempstead, and Truitt 2019; Roberts 1998). In explaining the meaning of "talking back," bell hooks (1989, 9) says, "Moving from silence into speech is for the oppressed, the colonized, the exploited, and those who stand and struggle side by side a gesture of defiance that heals, that makes new life and new growth possible. It is that act of speech, of 'talking back' that is no mere gesture of empty words, that is the expression of our movement from object to subject—the liberated voice."

Therefore, we believe that Black feminist autoethnography provides a more personal context and illustrates how we can authentically express ourselves in our diverse, intersectional experiences during the COVID-19 pandemic. We share five autoethnographic vignettes from the authors (Dawson, Green, Okoroma, Jackson, and Funmilayo). The authors of these vignettes were asked to reflect on their personal experiences during COVID-19 and the challenges and triumphs they navigated. The authors started their writing process in May 2020 and continuously reflected on how their own experiences were framed within Black feminist thought. In each vignette, the author describes her positionality and reflects on her lived experience. Before each vignette or cluster of vignettes, we present an analytic summary of key themes based on the tenets of Black feminist thought.

Through Our Looking Glass: Five Black Feminist Authoethnographic Vignettes

A central tenet of Black feminist thought calls for Black women to empower themselves by creating self-definitions and self-valuations that enable them to establish positive images and repel negative representations of Black women (Hill Collins 2009). In vignettes 1 (Green) and 2 (Dawson), the authors suggest that while COVID-19 shelter-in-place orders may have initially brought the hope of rest to some Black women who were able to work from home, it exacerbated the stressors associated with their existing roles and responsibilities. The reality is that since long before the pandemic, Black women have historically and systematically been overworked and underpaid, and they often return home to a "third shift" involving household labor and caregiving responsibilities (Power 2020; National Partnership for Women and Families 2022; Cohen et al. 2019; Jackson and Stewart 2003). Vignettes 1 and 2 provide illustrations consistent with available research suggesting that Black women, compared to their white counterparts, tend to spend more time caregiving and give higher levels of care (Cohen et al. 2019). Further, these Black women's stories underscore how Black women with jobs that afford flexibility still may not be able to fully reap the benefits of this privilege during the pandemic. Related, Black women's tendency to be informal caregivers also means that they may be in greater proximity to death and dying during the pandemic (Moore et al. 2020), referenced in vignette 2. In normal circumstances, Black women and their families can exercise cultural and spiritual practices that aid in the grief process while surrounding their dying loved ones. However, social distancing and limited visitation policies have disrupted families' ability to receive and provide social support to their loved ones, which can cause severe mental and emotional distress (Moore et al. 2020).

Noteworthy in the first two vignettes is the desire for and denial of rest among Black women (Harris-Lacewell 2001; Herbert Harris et al. 2018), and the intensification of this tension during the pandemic. The vignettes also discuss the stress and burden associated with role strain during the pandemic and describe how they reject controlling images or schemas. For example, the authors indicate contention with the Superwoman schema (characterized by feeling obligated to present an image of strength or suppress emotions, or to help others and succeed despite limited resources) (Woods-Giscombé 2010) and the Mammy archetype (characterized as a desexualized, maternal figure that puts the needs of all others before her own) (West 1995). The authors describe their liberation and resistance, which involve an intentional effort to recenter and redefine their roles with an eye to what success in their roles can and will look like.

Vignette 1: "Organized Chaos"

It is easy to have distinctions between your work life and your home life when they take place in two very different settings, but what happens when both environments blend together? I identify as an African American woman born and raised in a predominately white neighborhood. My lived experiences include being a first-generation college student fully immersed in African American culture while attending a historically Black college and university (HBCU). My parents were raised in poor country communities with limited access to financial and educational opportunities, making the inherent need to obtain financial and educational knowledge extremely difficult. I am a wife and a mother to three children, and I am also a college professor focused on health disparities and maternal and child health. I would describe my life before COVID-19 as organized chaos. Before the pandemic, both my husband and I worked outside of the home with three very active children, and we went from one activity to the next, one class to the next, and one project to the next. We are also caregivers to my elderly parents and are constantly shuffling them to doctors' appointments.

I thought the restrictions that COVID-19 placed on our daily activities would give me the rest I desperately needed, but the stress COVID-19 imposed was worse than I could have imagined. The onset of COVID-19 shelter-in-place orders drastically changed our daily shuffle of activities. First, I took on assisting my children with their virtual learning while they were at home. After about two weeks of social distancing, my mindset shifted from focusing just on their schoolwork to being concerned about their mental health. It was a constant struggle to find the words to ease their worries and find activities to keep their minds distracted from what was happening in the world. We started cooking as a family, picking new movies to enjoy at least twice a week, and participating in TikTok challenges to ease their minds and lighten the mood.[1]

In my professional life, I went from having my own office on campus where I could gather my thoughts, tend to my grading, and make a to-do list for the day, to throwing those to-do lists out the window because I had to add so many things on a daily basis that they became pointless. I started sharing a home office with my husband and navigating his virtual meeting schedule while going back and forth with my children to ensure they didn't miss a class meeting. The six-to-eight-hour workday I was accustomed to quickly turned into a twelve-to-fourteen-hour workday with the need to restructure classes to an online format and hold class meetings online during times when I could kick everyone else out of the office. The list of tasks that I was now responsible for seemed never ending, making it difficult for me to feel like I successfully accomplished anything on a daily basis. At any given moment, I was a mom, professor, caretaker, wife, cook, housekeeper, chauffer, triage nurse, toy builder, counselor, daughter, sister, or friend, and sometimes I took on all these roles at the same time. It was exhausting. The distinct roles that I had in place to mitigate the complexities of life and create clear lines of separation between work and life started to blur amid COVID-19 and forced me to re-create those roles and my standards of achievement in those roles. I found ways to accomplish multiple tasks and take on several roles simultaneously. I could cook a meal in the kitchen while helping my daughter with her homework at the counter and schedule a doctor's appointment for my parents at the same time. It was not ideal, but everything was being checked off my to-do list, which was still a measure of success for me.

In addition to re-creating my roles, refining my responsibilities, and making accommodations to my measures of success, I also had to focus on the mental struggles introduced by COVID-19. I am an introvert and absolutely love time alone to recharge and focus. How do you focus and recharge when people are surrounding you twenty-four seven? How could I provide my children with the support they needed for their mental stability when I struggled with my own? I have heard some of my friends say that the social isolation imposed by COVID-19 was an introvert's dream. Still, between the endless list of responsibilities and the lack of opportunities to reset, it seemed like it was a losing battle. I reassessed how I obtain my peace and my alone time to address this issue. That included waking up an hour before everyone to focus on my daily tasks and setting clear boundaries for bedtimes so that I had some time to recharge in the evenings.

—*Brandie Green*

Vignette 2: "Self-Advocacy"

My experience with self-advocacy and the pandemic makes me reflect on my great Aunteen's passing. She laid in her bed for two weeks suffering from symptoms of COVID-19 as her son, who lived in a spare room, continued to socialize. Questions formulated in my mind after I learned the details of her passing. Why didn't she ask anyone for help, or why didn't anyone, including her son, do more to help her? Did she put her identity of being a mother before her well-being? After three weeks, my great Aunteen was admitted to the hospital, and two days later, she died . . . alone. I'd rather not have my great Aunteen's death be a cautionary tale of Black matriarchy. Instead, my goal is to have her lived life, my life, be one of many oral histories passed down through generations showcasing the significance of self-advocacy.

As a cis woman of color, mother, and educator, I have felt the fight between role strain and self-advocacy. Before motherhood, I identified role strain only in the confines of networking within my career path and managing my finances. During COVID-19, my role strain is about mentally surviving. Even though my career has brought privileges of working from home, the intersectionality of my identities has collided, especially as I am seen as "always available" to the outside world. For example, now that I am working from home, my daughter is attached to my hip as I juggle work, motherhood, and caring for my spouse and parents.

Additionally, with many universities moving toward virtual engagement, many students are unaware that normative work hours still exist and have expectations that their needs will be met with high priority any time during the day. As I wish I could meet the demands of students seeking mentorship from a professional who self-identifies as they do, I am unsure how I can express in a professional manner that I'm exhausted. I'm exhausted because I'm in a consistent mode of fight-or-flight-or-freeze due to my phenotype(s), matrescence (the ever-changing landscape of motherhood), and life-work (im)balance. Not only am I experiencing emotional hijacking due to my increased anxiety of COVID-19 itself, but the pandemic has increased my attentiveness and numbness to my lived experiences. For example, the globalization of the #BlackLivesMatter movement has redefined my environment and has made me ultra-aware of my safe spaces and safe people. I'm finding myself being identified and self-identifying with the Mammy stereotype (caregiver to all) as I care for both my daughter and my aging parents (the sandwich generation). As an educator, I am experiencing a great divide between valid COVID-19 reports, the people whom those reports represent, and the question of how to make effective changes in my life to self-advocate. How do we advocate for ourselves, our families, and our communities if what is being provided to us (communities of color) as a mass audience does not include us (people who identify within the African Diaspora)? My mind wanders into a space of high anxiety when I speculate what the future world will look like for my child. How do I care for my aging parents? Can I be supportive while supervising my staff remotely? I find myself in various caretaker roles while failing to check in with my mental health. What is happening to my self-advocacy?

My saving grace has been increased stillness, along with daily intentions, routine, mindfulness, and reflective work. The pandemic has allowed me to move slower and with more intention, turning my energy inward. My best tool has been an Excel spreadsheet broken down hour by hour that reminds me to eat and take breaks. Every morning my alarm reminds me to stretch and take my medications. At night I have another alarm that makes me accountable for starting my bedtime routine and practicing a ten-minute meditation. In a chaotic world, I've had to slow down and refine my identities to include living in the present moment while attending to my cultural rites of religion and solidarity. For example, my Buddhist upbringing has reminded me that control is an illusion and that I should enjoy the present moment. Solidarity comes in the form of my professional counseling and community . . . my tribe of women experiencing parenthood, whom I can lean on. My coping mechanisms tied with faith and virtual community support illustrate a need for public health discourses to promote self-advocacy for women of color in a world that encourages us to fight against multiple oppressions.

—*Kenyatta Dawson*

A second tenet of Black feminist thought is that Black women recognize a distinct cultural and spiritual heritage that gives them the energy and skills to resist and transform daily struggles or discrimination (Hill Collins 2009). According to Audre Lorde (1988, 131), "caring for [oneself] is not self-indulgence. It is self-preservation, and that is an act of political warfare." In vignettes 3 (Jackson) and 4 (Funmilayo), the authors share experiences of role strain similar to the earlier vignettes. Mental health and well-being have been cited in the research as chief concerns among Black women during the pandemic (Gur et al. 2020; Jackson and Pederson 2020). Against the backdrop of the available scientific literature, vignettes 3 and 4 illustrate how Black women recognize and draw on their cultural and spiritual practices for self-empowerment, self-preservation, and restoration. In addition, the authors describe the importance of creating (physical and digital) space to be in community with family and other Black women. This represents the resistance to the multiple oppressive systems that create strenuous conditions Black women must live in and navigate—even during a pandemic.

Vignette 3: "I Knew I Had to Make a Change"

I identify as an African American, Christian woman born and raised in the rural part of Alabama to parents who only obtained a high school education. My parents were raised in poor country communities with limited access to financial and educational opportunities; however, both instilled in me the importance of earning a degree to position myself for careers outside of farming, entry-level nursing, or construction. Because of my parents' background, I made education a priority, attending college for a bachelor's and a master's degree. I am also an educator who instills the value of learning and is committed to assisting my students in living up to their fullest potential.

Since COVID-19, I can relate more to my students. Because I grew up in a rural area and my family did not have the financial means to afford extra luxuries such as the Internet and cable, I understand the struggles of not having the necessary tools to complete assignments and to stay as competitive as my peers. After the university suspended on-campus instruction, I learned that a substantive number of students did not have laptops or even the course's required textbooks. Others had a computer at home, but it was a family computer. Parents using the family computer took precedence as they had to work to support the family.

For me, an educator with no children, this really pulled at my heartstrings. The motherly instinct instilled in some women for centuries instantly kicked in. However, my stress level was high as I tried to help find resources, motivate, encourage, and re-create degree plans to keep students on track for graduation. Since COVID-19, my normal eight-to-nine-hour days quickly turned into fourteen-to-fifteen-hour days. When I started working from home, there was no clear separation between home and work. Before, I was able to leave my students and work issues at work. This is no longer available to me in the same way.

My breaking point came two months after I started working from home. I carried the weight of work constantly because I could not separate work from home. So, I began to experience anxiety, depression, and insomnia. One morning while logging into my work computer, I started crying and could not stop. But I could not articulate why. All I knew was that I was tired. At that point, I knew I had to make a change. So, I went back to the one thing I can always rely on—my faith. I began setting time aside for prayer and devotion. I fervently let my request be known to God. In my prayer time, he whispered, "balance, boundaries, and self-care." I started updating my calendar and intentionally setting aside breaks, prayer time, yoga, meditation, and even lunch! Yes, I was working through lunch. I also made task lists and prioritized my work in a way that would prevent me from working beyond my eight-hour shift. I had to learn that an empty lantern cannot give light. If I am not mentally, emotionally, and physically healthy, I cannot wholeheartedly assist my students or even myself.

—*Courtney Jackson*

Vignette 4: "The Sweetness of Faith"

I am an American-born, Nigerian-raised, Nigerian American, African American woman by destiny. I have been married for twenty years. I am a homeschool mom, a public health nutrition professional and a certified food literacy educator by qualification, an entrepreneur by choice, a student by occupation, a writer by heart, and a Muslim by soul.

My March calendar was full long before the World Health Organization declared COVID-19 as a pandemic. I had plans to attend my son's college health fair, to attend the weekly Friday services at my nearby Islamic centers, to participate in the upcoming speech contest at my local Toastmasters Club, to attend the travel club at my library, and to travel along with my family to North Carolina for spring break. All my plans came to a halt when the shelter-in-place orders were announced. Anxiety, confusion, disappointment, fear, helplessness, and stress all kicked in at once.

My Islamic faith has kept me going since this pandemic began. As the reality of the situation started unfolding, I was determined to change my mindset from a state of worry, panic, and fear to a state of total submission to the will of God, who knows all and sees all. I find comfort in my daily prayers and in the words of the Qur'an, the spiritual guidebook for Muslims. I lean on God to strengthen me and everyone throughout this ordeal. I listen to daily spiritual reminders and attend virtual prayer sermons and sister circles. I participate in webinars regarding public health issues. In addition, keeping in touch with my kith and kin, extended family members, neighbors, friends, and colleagues plays a crucial role in helping me maintain my spirituality and reminds me of the importance of fellowship, even if we cannot see one another.

The reality is that I sometimes find myself feeling down and restless. On such days, I succumb to my vulnerabilities and find myself missing that inner strength to remain calm and positive. When I realize this low moment, since writing helps me destress and unwind my cluttered mind, I write freely in my journal. As a Muslim, I find a sense of tranquility in reciting the verses of the Qur'an and pondering their meanings and how they relate to me. The verses usher in a sense of hope, and I am reminded by verse 28 in chapter 13, which states: "Truly, in the remembrance of God do hearts find rest." Sharing my spiritual exercises with my family, my Qur'an teacher, and a sisters-only online Qur'an study group gives me a sense of relief, even if short lived. These support systems keep me focused and remind me to have an attitude of gratitude during uncertainties. Consequently, having this kind of positive attitude prepares my body, mind, soul, and spirit for something bigger than myself, and that is Ramadan.

Ramadan, known as the month of fasting, was unique in every way during the COVID-19 pandemic. I will never forget Ramadan in 2020. Instead of the usual hype and celebratory preparations that occur worldwide to usher in the blessed month of Ramadan, a sense of sadness resonated in many Muslim homes and communities. I felt lonely without my community. Even though I fasted with my family, I missed the communal fasting and breaking of the fast at the Islamic centers around me. In a year buzzing with a pandemic, Muslims continued to fast and partake in various remote spiritual activities. I tuned in to podcasts and participated in Zoom meetings for spiritual upliftment during the month of Ramadan. I empathized with my children because this was their first time experiencing a different kind of Ramadan. As a Black Muslim mother, I had no other choice but to lean on my faith for solace and refuge, to be strong for my children. I continued to remind myself that this life experience was a test, and it was necessary to succeed during such a test. Otherwise, all hopes would be lost. But I could not do this alone; I needed more spiritual strength to keep me sane and grounded. I needed to be closer to my Creator and seek his help. I needed to assimilate the verses of the Qur'an and submit willingly.

I want other Black women to realize and know that keeping up with one's spirituality for inner strength as a Black woman during COVID-19 is a daily struggle. COVID-19 or not, our spiritual health fluctuates, and that is normal. Also, to truly taste the sweetness of faith in our isolated moments during COVID-19, it is essential to connect with family, friends, and other Black women. This is important not only for our spiritual health but also for our overall well-being. During the last ten months (March to December 2020), I have kept busy by reminiscing about my cultural heritage through storytelling, singing children's songs in my native Nigerian Yoruba language, and studying Arabic, French, and Twi languages. Meditating during my early morning walks around my neighborhood after the dawn prayers and keeping up with my graduate school classes also boost my physical and intellectual health. All these combined have a positive effect on one's spirituality.

Despite my struggles during this pandemic, I know that the impact has disproportionately hit many Black women here and abroad. Hence, as a Black woman, I have twofold goals: to uplift the lives and voices of Black women, here and in the Diaspora, through sisterly mentorship and empowerment, and to bring their lived experiences to life through grassroots advocacy and ethnographic research.

—*Maryam O. Funmilayo*

In 2020, Black immigrant women attending college in the United States experienced the threat of deportation amid the COVID-19 pandemic. In July, the U.S. Immigration and Customs Enforcement announced guidelines to deny visas to international students attending U.S. colleges and universities that had decided to offer online-only courses in the Fall 2020 semester (Larkin 2020). Although the policy was later revoked after public outcry, international students were still left to deal with the stress and fear of deportation (Chin 2020). Vignette 5 (Okoroma) helps illustrate how Black international students, much like Black U.S. domestic students, may navigate multiple structures of oppression. While the U.S. higher education system benefits from international students' academic, cultural, and economic contributions to its classrooms and local communities (National Association of Foreign Student Advisors 2019; Reuters 2020), international students are often marginalized by institutional and federal policies (Phillips 2001). For instance, institutional policies restrict how much international students can work and subsequently earn (despite having to pay federal and state taxes), and federal policies restrict international students' access to local financial assistance opportunities or even COVID-related aid from the government (Pesci 2020; U.S. Internal Revenue Service, n.d.; U.S. Department of Education 2020). Commonly reported challenges and experiences among Black international students include the complicated process of obtaining (and retaining) visas, the difficulty in being separated from family (for those students who don't have family stateside), and the need to find community through shared culture and identity (George Mwangi and English 2017; Caldwell and Hyams-Ssekasi 2016). In the final vignette, the author shares her experience navigating the pandemic as an international student at a U.S. university. The author's story demonstrates the importance of recognizing how the pandemic exacerbates existing policies' adverse effects (rooted in structural oppression) on Black international students. In particular, the author's story brings forth two questions: what are the inherent biases entrenched in COVID-19-related policy decisions at the federal, local, and institutional levels, and how do these policies create oppressive (or restorative) circumstances that Black international students must navigate during the pandemic?

Vignette 5: A Dream Deferred and a Vision Realized

I identify as a Nigerian woman born and raised in Lagos, Nigeria. My parents received their higher education in Nigeria but had plans for my brother and me to study abroad as an opportunity to learn from other cultures. It was always my mother's dream for my siblings and me to go to college in the United States. She would always say, "I cannot wait to see my baby walk across the stage with honors!" When I started college in fall 2016, I promised her that I would make her and my dad proud by finishing college with the highest honors. As I think back to early January 2020, when COVID-19 seemed like a distant problem, I was truly looking forward to starting the academic year. It was my last semester in college, everything was going according to plan, and I was excited about the opportunity to see my parents at my graduation ceremony.

In mid-March 2020, my friends and I left campus for spring break, not knowing that it would be the last time (at least for a while) that we could gather for class and spend quality time together. During spring break, my university announced a one-week extension to the break along with COVID-19 shelter-in-place orders and a plan to transition all classes online. The thought of this drastic change was frightening because I lived on campus, and I was not sure of what this change meant for me. Also, I specifically chose an on-campus degree program because I prefer to learn in a physical classroom and to interact with faculty and classmates. Therefore, the transition from face-to-face classes to online classes was challenging. For example, it was difficult staying focused during class sessions, especially classes that were more than two hours long, while in the comfort of my home. Also, managing and coordinating group work with classmates was already a challenge before the pandemic, but trying to do this virtually and under chronic stress was more difficult.

As if the turmoil of online classes was not enough, the bad news just kept coming. First, the university announced that graduation ceremonies would have to be postponed. Second, the U.S. government announced that international travel had to be suspended for everyone's safety. This policy was also followed by the U.S. government enacting a now-revised rule that international students had to show they would be taking at least one in-person course despite the reality that most universities had transitioned all their courses to online. This left me in a state of hopelessness. What was supposed to be one of the best times of my life quickly turned out to be one of the worst.

I did not have the opportunity to fly back to Nigeria to quarantine with my family, so I stayed on campus. I felt dejected, and watching others have their immediate families to rely on during this time hurt me more. When May 2020 came, the school hosted an online ceremony for graduating students. This was not what I wanted or expected. Some of my classmates and their families could plan creative, physically distant graduation celebrations. This was difficult to watch because I did not get the opportunity to celebrate with family in person, even in a distanced way. I met my goal of graduating summa cum laude, but my promise to my parents was only partially fulfilled.

Overall, I gained many insights through my personal experiences during the pandemic, coupled with my professional perspective gained through my recent bachelor's degree in public health. As a future public health professional, I am inspired to find better ways to address infectious diseases while also considering the social context of groups, including Black students, who may experience difficulties navigating public health emergencies. For example, many students faced major financial difficulties during the pandemic. International students were not eligible for financial assistance, which meant they had to work harder to find other opportunities to support themselves while also completing their educational programs. As a future epidemiologist, I am positioned to better understand the importance of elevating and centering the voices of those most affected by COVID-19 and future public health emergencies.

—*Chizoba Uzoamaka Okoroma*

Our Whole Story

This chapter aimed to center Black women's voices and experiences during the pandemic using Black feminist autoethnography. Using autoethnographic vignettes, we created our own "looking glass," allowing us to engage in self-definition, self-curation, and resistance collectively. Bringing together this collection of Black women's voices has allowed us to accomplish three goals. First, it empowers us to resist hegemonic empirical models that attempt to tell Black women's stories in fragmented and incomplete ways. Empirical literatures rooted in white supremacy have, in many ways, defined which of Black women's intersectional identities are worthy of attention (e.g., the overrepresentation of research on poor Black women). There is a need to present women as whole, especially in empirical spaces where fragmented, incomplete stories of Black women are often told. These autoethnographic vignettes allow us to present Black women in a holistic, intersectional manner.

Second, and related, this collection of Black women's voices illustrates the multiple "interlocking" intersections at which Black women in the United States are situated (Hill Collins 2009; Crenshaw 1989). It is at these intersections that Black women must navigate and resist the downstream effects of systems of oppression that are intensified by the COVID-19 pandemic. In focusing on these intersections, we illustrate the shared and nuanced experiences of Black women during the pandemic. For instance, the autoethnographic vignettes speak of common experiences of stress and resilience through self-empowerment and social and spiritual resources during the pandemic. There are also lived experiences that are uniquely tied due to nativity or immigration status, maternal status, and caregiving roles and expectations.

Finally, this collection of Black women's voices allows us to tell a whole story that can aid in achieving health equity. Black women's whole stories related to mental health, role and caregiver strain, social and spiritual resources, immigration status, or grief during the pandemic can contribute to developing tailored, contextually responsive COVID-19 preventive interventions. Further, although quantitative data regarding Black women's experiences during the pandemic are useful, there is a need for more research that provides in-depth, intersectional explorations into Black women's experiences (e.g., role strain, caregiving, mothering, etc.) during the pandemic. Research into these experiences will contribute to a growing literature providing holistic views of Black women's lives during the pandemic. In terms of policymaking, there is certainly a need to promote equitable COVID-19 testing, vaccination, and treatment access among Black women at multiple intersections. However, since the effects of existing policies, rooted in gendered racism, have been exacerbated during the COVID-19 pandemic, there is additionally a need for policies that ensure high-quality health-care access, optimal working conditions, housing stability, immigration equity during and beyond public health emergencies, and food security for Black women. Based on our collection of vignettes and the current literature, future COVID-19 policymaking efforts should consider the disproportionate impact of COVID-19 on Black women's mental and physical health care as well as their social, educational, and work environments. This approach to policymaking is key because it emphasizes the systems and environments that need to be changed rather than attempting to change Black women.

Black women's whole story must be centered if we are to see progress toward health equity. Black feminist methodologies, such as Black feminist autoethnography, provide vehicles through which Black women can actively use their voices to inform equitable public health solutions during and after the COVID-19 pandemic (Hill Collins 2009; hooks 1989; Davis 2018; Isoke 2013). We hope that our voices and stories shared in this chapter will contribute to the growing literatures centered on Black women's lived experiences during the COVID-19 pandemic and inform research, prevention, and policy-making efforts to benefit Black women.

Notes

We note several authorial decisions. First, we, the authors, often use "we" in this chapter, which sometimes expands to include our perspectives as Black women scholars, practitioners, and students who, in accordance with the Black feminist paradigm, actively participate in knowledge generation through our lived experiences. Second, due to space limitations, we focus primarily on COVID-19 in the U.S. context. Many examples that we share or cite derive primarily from the United States, although occasionally, we use some worldwide examples. Finally, our definition of Black women refers to a sociopolitical collective identity and encompasses African Diasporic women regardless of proximity to the continent. Our definition of Black women also encompasses and embraces the intersecting diversity of this group in terms of gender identity and expression, sexual orientation, socioeconomic position, religion, culture, and national origin.

1. TikTok is a video-sharing social media platform used to make and share short video clips from genres like dance/entertainment, comedy, and education.

References

Anurudran, Ashri, Leah Yared, Cameron Comrie, Katherine Harrison, and Thomas Burke. 2020. "Domestic Violence amid COVID-19." *International Journal of Gynecology and Obstetrics* 150 (2): 255–56.

Armitage, Richard, and Laura B. Nellums. 2020. "The COVID-19 Response Must Be Disability Inclusive." *Lancet Public Health* 5 (5): article e257. https://doi.org/10.1016/S2468-2667(20)30076-1.

Bailey, Zinzi D., Nancy Krieger, Madina Agénor, Jasmine Graves, Natalia Linos, and Mary T. Bassett. 2017. "Structural Racism and Health Inequities in the USA: Evidence and Interventions." *Lancet* 389 (10077): 1453–63.

Baker, Marissa G., Trevor K. Peckham, and Noah S. Seixas. 2020. "Estimating the Burden of United States Workers Exposed to Infection or Disease: A Key Factor in Containing Risk of COVID-19 Infection." *PLOS ONE* 15 (4): article e0232452. https://doi.org/10.1371/journal.pone.0232452.

BMJ Gender Diversity Group. 2020. "Where Are the Women Experts on Covid-19? Mostly Missing." *BMJ Opinion* (blog), June 25, 2020. https://blogs.bmj.com/bmj/2020/06/25/where-are-the-women-experts-on-covid-19-mostly-missing/.

Bowleg, Lisa. 2020. "We're Not All in This Together: On COVID-19, Intersectionality, and Structural Inequality." *American Journal of Public Health* 110 (7): 917.

Brown Speights, Joedrecka S., Alexandra C. H. Nowakowski, Jessica De Leon, M. Miaisha Mitchell, and Ivana Simpson. 2017. "Engaging African American Women in Research: An Approach to Eliminate Health Disparities in the African American Community." *Family Practice* 34 (3): 322–29.

Brown-Vincent, Layla D. 2019. "Seeing It for Wearing It: Autoethnography as Black Feminist Methodology." *Taboo* 18 (1): 109–25.

Caldwell, Elizabeth Frances, and Denis Hyams-Ssekasi. 2016. "Leaving Home: The Challenges of Black-African International Students Prior to Studying Overseas." *Journal of International Students* 6 (2): 588–613.

Chambers, Brittany D., Helen A. Arega, Silvia E. Arabia, Brianne Taylor, Robyn G. Barron, Brandi Gates, Loretta Scruggs-Leach, Karen A. Scott, and Monica R. McLemore. 2021. "Black Women's Perspectives on Structural Racism Across the Reproductive Lifespan: A Conceptual Framework for Measurement Development." *Maternal and Child Health Journal* 25: 402–13.

Chandler, Rasheeta, Dominique Guillaume, Andrea G. Parker, Amber Mack, Jill Hamilton, Jemea Dorsey, and Natalie D. Hernandez. 2021. "The Impact of COVID-19 Among Black Women: Evaluating Perspectives and Sources of Information." *Ethnicity and Health* 26 (1): 80–93.

Chang, Heewon. 2008. *Autoethnography as Method*. Walnut Creek, Calif.: Left Coast Press.

Chin, Monica. 2020. "The ICE Directive Is Gone, but International Students Still Fear Deportation." *Verge*, August 18, 2020. https://www.theverge.com/21365223/ice-international-students-college-coronavirus-covid-19-school-year.

Chishlom, Jamiyla. 2020. "COVID-19 Creates Added Danger for Women in Homes with Domestic Violence." *Colorlines*, March 27, 2020. https://www.colorlines.com/articles/covid-19-creates-added-danger-women-homes-domestic-violence.

Cohen, Steven A., Natalie J. Sabik, Sarah K. Cook, Ariana B. Azzoli, and Carolyn A. Mendez-Luck. 2019. "Differences Within Differences: Gender Inequalities in Caregiving Intensity Vary by Race and Ethnicity in Informal Caregivers." *Journal of Cross-Cultural Gerontology* 34 (3): 245–63.

Connor, Jade, Sarina Madhavan, Mugdha Mokashi, Hanna Amanuel, Natasha R. Johnson, Lydia E. Pace, and Deborah Bartz. 2020. "Health Risks and Outcomes That Disproportionately Affect Women During the Covid-19 Pandemic: A Review." *Social Science and Medicine* 266: article 113364. https://doi.org/10.1016/j.socscimed.2020.113364.

Crenshaw, Kimberlé. 1989. "Demarginalizing the Intersection of Race and Sex: A Black Feminist Critique of Antidiscrimination Doctrine, Feminist Theory and Antiracist Politics." *University of Chicago Legal Forum*, no. 18, 139–67.

Davis, Olga Idriss. 1999. "In the Kitchen: Transforming the Academy Through Safe Spaces of Resistance." *Western Journal of Communication* 63 (3): 364–81.

Davis, Shardé M. 2018. "Taking Back the Power: An Analysis of Black Women's Communicative Resistance." *Review of Communication* 18 (4): 301–18.

Doll, Kemi M., Bridgette Hempstead, and Anjali R. Truitt. 2019. "Seeking Black Women's Voices in Endometrial Cancer Research via Deliberate Community Engagement." *Progress in Community Health Partnerships: Research, Education, and Action* 13 (3): 253–64.

Feinberg, Lynn, Susan Reinhard, Ari Houser, and Rita Choula. 2011. "Valuing the Invaluable: 2011 Update: The Growing Contributions and Costs of Family Caregiving." AARP Public Policy Institute: Insight on the Issues. https://assets.aarp.org/rgcenter/ppi/ltc/i51-caregiving.pdf.

Frye, Jocelyn. 2020. "On the Frontlines at Work and at Home: The Disproportionate Economic Effects of the Coronavirus Pandemic on Women of Color." Center for American Progress. April 23, 2020. https://www.americanprogress.org/article/frontlines-work-home/.

Garg, Shikha. 2020. "Hospitalization Rates and Characteristics of Patients Hospitalized with Laboratory-Confirmed Coronavirus Disease 2019—COVID-NET, 14 States, March 1–30, 2020." *Morbidity and Mortality Weekly Report* 69 (15): 458–64.

Garza, Roseanna. 2020. "Health Officials: COVID-19 Shows Impact of Socio-economic Inequities." *San Antonio Report*, August 12, 2020. https://san antonioreport.org/health-officials-covid-19-shows-impact-of-socioeconomic -inequities/.

Gausman, Jewel, and Ana Langer. 2020. "Sex and Gender Disparities in the COVID-19 Pandemic." *Journal of Women's Health* 29 (4): 465–66.

Gee, Gilbert C., and Chandra L. Ford. 2011. "Structural Racism and Health Inequities." *Du Bois Review: Social Science Research on Race* 8 (1): 115–32.

Gee, Gilbert C., Marguerite J. Ro, and Anne W. Rimoin. 2020. "Seven Reasons to Care About Racism and COVID-19 and Seven Things to Do to Stop It." *American Journal of Public Health* 110 (7): 954–55.

George Mwangi, Chrystal A., and Shelvia English. 2017. "Being Black (and) Im-migrant Students: When Race, Ethnicity, and Nativity Collide." *International Journal of Multicultural Education* 19 (2): 100–130.

Gervasi, Angela. 2020. "How Language Can Be a Deadly COVID-19 Compli-cation for US Immigrants." *New Humanitarian*, July 30, 2020. https://www .thenewhumanitarian.org/news-feature/2020/07/30/coronavirus-immigrant -refugee-language.

Griffin, Rachel Alicia. 2012. "I AM an Angry Black Woman: Black Feminist Autoethnography, Voice, and Resistance." *Women's Studies in Communica-tion* 35 (2): 138–57.

Gur, Raquel E., Lauren K. White, Rebecca Waller, Ran Barzilay, Tyler M. Moore, Sara Kornfield, Wanjiku F.M. Njoroge et al. 2020. "The Disproportionate Bur-den of the COVID-19 Pandemic Among Pregnant Black Women." *Psychiatry Research* 293: article 113475. https://doi.org/10.1016/j.psychres.2020.113475.

Guy-Sheftall, Beverly, ed. 1995. *Words of Fire: An Anthology of African-American Feminist Thought*. New York: New Press.

Harcourt, Jennifer, Azaibi Tamin, Xiaoyan Lu, Shifaq Kamili, Senthil K. Sakthivel, Janna Murray, Krista Queen et al. 2020. "Severe Acute Respiratory Syn-drome Coronavirus 2 from Patient with Coronavirus Disease, United States." *Emerging Infectious Diseases Journal* 26 (6). https://doi.org/10.3201/eid2606 .200516.

Harris-Lacewell, Melissa. 2001. "No Place to Rest." *Women and Politics* 23 (3): 1–33. https://doi.org/10.1300/J014v23n03_01.

Herbert Harris, Eboni T., DeAnne K. Hillfinger Messias, Shirley M. Timmons, Tisha M. Felder, and Robin Dawson Estrada. 2018. "Rest Among African American Women: The Current State of the Science." *Holistic Nursing Prac-tice* 32 (3): 143–48.

Hill Collins, Patricia. 1996. "What's in a Name? Womanism, Black Feminism, and Beyond." *Black Scholar* 26 (1): 9–17.

Hill Collins, Patricia. 2009. *Black Feminist Thought: Knowledge, Consciousness, and the Politics of Empowerment.* New York: Routledge.

hooks, bell. 1989. *Talking Back: Thinking Feminist, Thinking Black.* Boston: South End Press.

Isoke, Zenzele. 2013. "Framing Black Women's Resistance: A Black Feminist Intersectional Approach." In *Urban Black Women and the Politics of Resistance*, edited by Zenzele Isoke, 13–36. New York: Palgrave Macmillan.

Jackson, Brandi, and Aderonke B. Pederson. 2020. "Facing Both Covid-19 and Racism, Black Women Are Carrying a Particularly Heavy Burden." *Washington Post*, September 4, 2020.

Jackson, Pamela Braboy, and Quincy Thomas Stewart. 2003. "A Research Agenda for the Black Middle Class: Work Stress, Survival Strategies, and Mental Health." *Journal of Health and Social Behavior* 44 (3): 442–55.

Jaiswal, J., C. LoSchiavo, and D. C. Perlman. 2020. "Disinformation, Misinformation and Inequality-Driven Mistrust in the Time of COVID-19: Lessons Unlearned from AIDS Denialism." *AIDS and Behavior* 24: 2776–80.

Johns Hopkins Coronavirus Resource Center. n.d. "COVID-19 Map." Accessed January 26, 2021. https://coronavirus.jhu.edu/map.html.

Kofman, Yasmin B., and Dana Rose Garfin. 2020. "Home Is Not Always a Haven: The Domestic Violence Crisis amid the COVID-19 Pandemic." *Psychological Trauma: Theory, Research, Practice, and Policy* 12 (S1): article S199. https://doi.org/10.1037/tra0000866.

Krug, Teresa. 2020. "Race to Translate COVID-19 Info as Some US Communities Left Out." *Aljazeera*, May 31, 2020. https://www.aljazeera.com/news/2020/3/31/race-to-translate-covid-19-info-as-some-us-communities-left-out.

Larkin, Max. 2020. "ICE Threatens To Deport International Students If They Don't Attend In-Person Classes." *All Things Considered*. National Public Radio, July 7, 2020. https://www.npr.org/2020/07/07/888510061/ice-threatens-to-deport-international-students-if-they-dont-attend-in-person-cla.

Laurencin, Cato T., and Aneesah McClinton. 2020. "The COVID-19 Pandemic: A Call to Action to Identify and Address Racial and Ethnic Disparities." *Journal of Racial and Ethnic Health Disparities* 7 (3): 398–402.

Lipscomb, Allen E., and Wendy Ashley. 2020. "Surviving Being Black and a Clinician During a Dual Pandemic: Personal and Professional Challenges in a Disease and Racial Crisis." *Smith College Studies in Social Work* 90 (4): 221–36.

Lorde, Audre. 1984. *Sister Outsider: Essays and Speeches*. Berkeley, Calif.: Crossing Press.

Lorde, Audre. 1988. *A Burst of Light: Essays*. Ithaca, N.Y.: Firebrand Books.

Louisias, Margee, and Lyndonna Marrast. 2020. "Intersectional Identity and Racial Inequality During the COVID-19 Pandemic: Perspectives of Black Physician Mothers." *Journal of Women's Health* 29 (9): 1148–49.

McDermott, Casey. 2020. "Black Women Are Affected Disproportionately by COVID-19 in N.H., New Data Shows." New Hampshire Public Radio, August 13, 2020. https://www.nhpr.org/post/black-women-are-affected-disproportionately-covid-19-nh-new-data-shows.

McLemore, Monica, mod. 2019. "#ListentoBlackWomen: A Community-Based Approach to Understand and Address Structural Racism." Panel discussion at the American Public Health Association, Philadelphia, Pa., November 5.

Mein, Stephen A. 2020. "COVID-19 and Health Disparities: The Reality of 'the Great Equalizer.'" *Journal of General Internal Medicine* 35 (8): 2439–40.

Moore, Sharon E., Sharon D. Jones-Eversley, Willie F. Tolliver, Betty L. Wilson, and Christopher A. Jones. 2020. "Six Feet Apart or Six Feet Under: The Impact of COVID-19 on the Black Community." *Death Studies* 46 (4): 891–901.

National Association of Foreign Student Advisors. 2019. "New NAFSA Data: Despite Stagnant Enrollment, International Students Contribute Nearly $41 Billion to the U.S. Economy." November 18, 2019. https://www.nafsa.org/about/about-nafsa/new-nafsa-data-despite-stagnant-enrollment.

National Center for Transgender Equality. 2020. "The Coronavirus (COVID-19) Guide." April 3, 2020. https://transequality.org/covid19.

National Partnership for Women and Families. 2022. "Quantifying America's Gender Wage Gap by Race/Ethnicity." January 2022. https://www.nationalpartnership.org/our-work/resources/economic-justice/fair-pay/quantifying-americas-gender-wage-gap.pdf.

Office for National Statistics. 2020. "Coronavirus (COVID-19) Related Deaths by Ethnic Group, England and Wales." May 7, 2020. https://www.ons.gov.uk/peoplepopulationandcommunity/birthsdeathsandmarriages/deaths/articles/coronavirusrelateddeathsbyethnicgroupenglandandwales/2march2020to10april2020.

OpenSAFELY Collaborative, Elizabeth Williamson, Alex J. Walker, Krishnan Bhaskaran, Seb Bacon, Chris Bates, Caroline E. Morton et al. 2020. "OpenSAFELY: Factors Associated with COVID-19-Related Hospital Death in the Linked Electronic Health Records of 17 Million Adult NHS Patients."

Preprint. MedRxiv. Uploaded May 7, 2020. https://doi.org/10.1101/2020.05
.06.20092999.

Pesci, Sasha. 2020. "Vulnerable and Undervalued: ICE Threatens to Disrupt the
Lives of International Students in the U.S." *Medium*, July 10, 2020. https://
medium.com/@spesci/.

Phillips, Kristin. 2001. "Moving Out of the Margins: Mattering and the International Student Experience." *Vermont Connection* 22 (1). https://scholarworks
.uvm.edu/tvc/vol22/iss1/7.

Power, Kate. 2020. "The COVID-19 Pandemic Has Increased the Care Burden
of Women and Families." *Sustainability: Science, Practice and Policy* 16 (1):
67–73.

Reed, Darius D. 2020. "Racial Disparities in Healthcare: How COVID-19 Rav-
aged One of the Wealthiest African American Counties in the United States."
Social Work in Public Health 36 (2): 118–27.

Reuters. 2020. "Explainer: What 1.1 Million Foreign Students Contribute to the
U.S. Economy." July 8, 2020. https://www.reuters.com/article/us-usa-immi
gration-students-economy-expl-idUSKBN2492VS.

Roberts, Dorothy. 1998. *Killing the Black Body: Race, Reproduction and the
Meaning of Liberty*. New York: Penguin Random House.

Schneider, Eric C. 2020. "Failing the Test—The Tragic Data Gap Undermin-
ing the U.S. Pandemic Response." *New England Journal of Medicine* 383 (4):
299–302.

Solomon, Mildred Z., Matthew K. Wynia, and Lawrence O. Gostin. 2020.
"Covid-19 Crisis Triage—Optimizing Health Outcomes and Disability Rights."
New England Journal of Medicine 383 (5): article e27. https://doi.org/10.1056
/NEJMp2008300.

Spates, Kamesha. 2012. "'The Missing Link': The Exclusion of Black Women
in Psychological Research and the Implications for Black Women's Mental
Health." *SAGE Open* 2 (3): article 2158244012455179. https://doi.org/10.1177
/2158244012455179.

Stokes, Erin K. 2020. "Coronavirus Disease 2019 Case Surveillance—United
States, January 22–May 30, 2020." *Morbidity and Mortality Weekly Report*
69 (24): 759–65.

Taylor, Keeanga-Yamahtta, ed. 2017. *How We Get Free: Black Feminism and the
Combahee River Collective*. Chicago: Haymarket Books.

U.S. Department of Education. 2020. "U.S. Department of Education Issues
Rule to Protect American Taxpayers from Waste, Fraud, and Abuse, Ensure
COVID-19 Relief Funds Get to Eligible Students." Press release, June 11, 2020.

U.S. Internal Revenue Service. n.d. "Taxation of Nonresident Aliens." Accessed January 23, 2021. https://www.irs.gov/individuals/international-taxpayers /taxation-of-nonresident-aliens.

Vavra, Joseph S. 2020. "Shutdown Sectors Represent Large Share of All US Employment." Becker Friedman Institute, March 27, 2020. https://bfi.uchi cago.edu/insight/finding/shutdown-sectors-represent-large-share-of-all-us -employment/.

West, Carolyn M. 1995. "Mammy, Sapphire, and Jezebel: Historical Images of Black Women and Their Implications for Psychotherapy." *Psychotherapy: Theory, Research, Practice, Training* 32 (3): 458–66.

Woods-Giscombé, Cheryl L. 2010. "Superwoman Schema: African American Women's Views on Stress, Strength, and Health." *Qualitative Health Research* 20 (5): 668–83.

CHAPTER 6

From Both Ends of the Table

A Differently Abled Black Woman and COVID-19

Radscheda Nobles

Tricia B. Bent-Goodley (2001) identifies women of color as more likely than others to experience discrimination when seeking help in crisis situations. Persons with disabilities, especially disabled persons of color, are invisible in research and our conversations around COVID-19. In popular media, the hashtag #DisabilityTooWhite proposes that discussion of disabled white persons has often significantly overshadowed that of other disabled groups (Thompson 2016). Researcher and scholar Christopher M. Bell (2011, 3) has even called for the disability research field to be renamed "white disability studies." And COVID-19 has shown yet another area in which Black disabled women disappear. In this chapter, using autoethnography, I disrupt the narratives of invisibility. In doing so, I speak from both ends of the table because I exist in the world as a researcher as well as the research subject. In qualitative research, the researcher takes on various roles within the research setting. According to Patricia A. Adler and Peter Adler (1994), in research, the roles can vary between fully participating in the group being analyzed (an insider) and being a stranger to the group being analyzed (an outsider). Insider researchers study a group to which they belong, whereas outsider researchers do not belong to the group under study (Unluer 2012). As a researcher and a differently abled Black woman, I am analyzing groups I belong to as an insider.

I identify as a single, Christian, and differently abled Black woman. I have visible and hidden conditions, including neurofibromatosis, epilepsy, post-traumatic stress disorder, depression, asthma, anxiety, a speech impairment, ADHD, and a learning disability. I was raised in a home with a stepfather and my mother, a Black woman with multiple health conditions who experienced violence. After my mother's death, I found myself sixteen years old and homeless. I obtained my GED and have been educating myself ever since. Now, you can call me Dr. Radscheda. My life and health conditions taught me about resilience. However, I must say that my resilience is being tested and that my health conditions never take a break, not even for the COVID-19 pandemic. Those of us with disabilities and chronic health conditions face pandemic challenges and additional stressors and barriers unique to us. Yet, as if that is not hard enough, many companies and institutions like my university have returned to an expectation of normalcy, requiring us to return to the prepandemic status quo, despite the ongoing pandemic. These ableist expectations that everyone can comply with mandates and unclear policies create dangerous situations for me and others with disabilities or health conditions. As a differently abled Black woman professor with health conditions, I am most terrified by the unknown. With this chapter, I hope to bring a deeper understanding to COVID-19, inclusion, and opportunities for at-risk populations, especially disabled women of color.

Impact of the COVID-19 Pandemic

COVID-19 appeared out of nowhere, and in just a few months, the pandemic dramatically changed the way many of us live and work. As infections swept the world, the virus contributed to enormous economic and physical burdens. Since early March 2020, the number of confirmed cases and deaths in the United States has risen considerably. As of January 2021, there were about 87,273,380 confirmed cases and 1,899,400 deaths worldwide (World Health Organization 2021). In the United States alone, between January 21, 2020, and January 11, 2021, there were 22,322,956 cases and 373,167 deaths (Centers for Disease Control and Prevention 2021). The pandemic has had a detrimental effect on those groups in the most vulnerable positions. In the United States, Black individuals and other minority groups are the hardest hit, with Black individuals accounting for a proportion of COVID deaths that is two or three times their proportion of the population (Williams 2020).

According to the Centers for Disease Control and Prevention (2019), African Americans make up 13 percent of the population and account for 34 percent of COVID-19 confirmed cases. African Americans and other minority groups are disproportionately affected by the pandemic in that they are infected, tested, hospitalized, and treated more than other groups (Sood and Vanita 2021). Disparities in COVID-19 outcomes for these groups are more likely due to the long-standing history of structural racism. Factors like poverty, mass incarceration, limited health-care access, limited access to healthy foods, and at-risk occupational exposures contribute to a greater predisposition to the virus.

Moreover, the COVID-19 pandemic exacerbated these preexisting disparities, especially for those who sit at the intersections of multiple and overlapping systems of oppression, such as homeless transgender adolescents or differently abled Black women. The pandemic presents a real and present threat to the lives of Black women and people with disabilities. Both are at a higher risk of severe illness and death from the virus. Lack of resources and support causes the crisis to heighten and makes the infection even deadlier. Black women are often unheard and obscured in research. In an interview, Black cardiologist Michelle Albert revealed, "Black women's experiences are lost in the wilderness, and they often receive the short stick in society" (Jordan 2020). As a result, the narratives of Black women and people with disabilities, particularly disabled people of color, are limited and told from a whitewashed, privileged, and ableist perspective. Given this, it is imperative to record and understand the COVID-19 experiences of vulnerable populations such as Black women and people with disabilities in order to ensure these populations' inclusion in research, public health recommendations, and policy.

Who Is Most at Risk for COVID-19?

Black women and people with disabilities sit at the center of overlapping systems of oppression that contribute to a wide range of health and quality of life outcomes and risks during the COVID-19 pandemic. Even before the pandemic, America has always had problems with those at the margins, such as Black women and those with disabilities or health conditions. The pandemic is a perfect storm for revealing these inequalities and compounding existing barriers rooted in ableism. The pandemic's fallout challenged many people, but some of us have fewer resources and support to help us cope. Not only do groups at the margins bear the burden of the coronavirus unfairly, but their mental and financial well-being are affected as well. While these groups share many experiences that make them more vulnerable to COVID-19, their burdens with the virus are exclusive. As COVID-19 once again reveals, as a Black woman with a disability, I get lost in data collection. As a result, I often have to piece together data to see myself. Below I offer a snapshot of the intersection of COVID-19, race, gender, and disability, recognizing that it does not tell a complete story. Let's look at people with disabilities, Black individuals, and Black women in turn, focusing on their experiences with COVID-19.

What Does It Mean to Be Black, Woman, and Disabled While Facing COVID-19?
People with Disabilities
Most individuals have general challenges with the pandemic; however, there are additional outcomes and barriers for individuals with

disabilities. Research on the specific impact of COVID-19 on people with disabilities is limited. In the United States, roughly one in four adults is living with a disability; sixty-one million Americans have a disability that affects major life activities (Okoro et al. 2018), which may heighten or exacerbate their experiences with COVID-19. Having a disability and impairment does not in itself entail a higher risk of COVID-19, but many people with disabilities and impairments have preexisting conditions that make the virus more dangerous for them (Lund et al., 2020; Sakellariou, Malfitano, and Rotarou 2020). The lives of people with disabilities and impairments are also jeopardized by the lack of access to COVID-19 testing.

Emerging research on COVID-19 and individuals with disabilities is limited; however, it shows that people with disabilities may face a more deadly COVID-19 outcome. People with disabilities, especially individuals living in care facilities, may be at higher risk from the pandemic. Data from a residential group home in New York reveal that people with intellectual disabilities and developmental disorders are three times more likely to die from the virus than people without these conditions (Landes et al. 2020). Scott D. Landes and colleagues (2020) found this was mainly due to their not being able to communicate effectively. Like other studies on COVID-19 and disability, this study did not disaggregate COVID-19 outcomes by race and gender.

Furthermore, additional barriers can present ongoing and unique challenges for people with disabilities and impairments. Individuals with disabilities are more likely to live in poverty, be unemployed, and experience higher rates of violence, abuse, and neglect. People with disabilities and impairments have been historically marginalized, oppressed, and viewed as less than by society (Petersilia 2001). Often persons with disabilities are rejected when they attempt to gain employment. Disabled persons with jobs are more likely to lose jobs and experience difficulties returning to work (Mitra and Kruse 2016). All of this is compounded during the era of COVID-19.

Individuals with disabilities also face barriers to accessing critical needs for support and resources. Data show that people with disabilities find it difficult to obtain needed medical supplies, which is even more problematic during a pandemic (Campbell et al. 2009). Stay-at-home orders caused people with disabilities and impairments to lose access to caregivers and service providers. Some people with disabilities cannot isolate themselves like others. Support workers may not be willing to risk bringing the virus back to their own home, thus leaving the family responsible for the disabled individuals' care. The lack of caregivers and service providers puts people with disabilities and impairments in danger, raising the risk of neglect and abuse. Studies have also shown that social distancing among people with disabilities and impairments may intensify loneliness during the pandemic. Compared to nondisabled individuals, people with disabilities report higher social isolation levels (O'Sullivan and Bourgoin 2010). As a result of exacerbating poverty and prolonged isolation, COVID-19 has increased depression and cognitive, physical, and mental health issues (Lund et al. 2020). More data are needed on rates of infection, hospitalization, outcomes, and death disaggregated by disability, age, race, gender, and income to better understand and evaluate the impact of COVID-19 on multiple vulnerable groups.

Black Individuals

Black individuals are bearing the brunt of COVID-19. In the United States, compared to their white counterparts, Black individuals are at higher risk for many illnesses and diseases; COVID-19 is no different. Data show that Black individuals are disproportionately infected with COVID-19, and that they are more than four times more likely to die from COVID-19 than are their white counterparts (Dyer 2020). The Centers for Disease Control and Prevention (2019) reported that Black people account for about 25 percent of all people hospitalized with COVID-19. The Black community has higher rates of impact due to limited health-care access, poverty rates, high mass incarceration rates, and other detrimental factors (Laurencin and Walker 2020).

Furthermore, many states implemented stay-at-home orders to contain the spread of the virus. However, many Black individuals, employed by businesses deemed essential, could not remain at home safely. Data indicate that those who are Black, or members of other minority groups are overrepresented in "essential" work, and they are more likely than others to be exposed to COVID-19 while working in settings such as gas stations, grocery stores, and the transportation industry (Bozarth and Hanks 2020). Many such individuals working in critical positions are less likely to have insurance. According to Janis V. Sanchez-Hucles (1997), Black individuals are more likely to have low-paying jobs that do not allow them flexibility, health insurance, or paid medical leave.

Black Women

Unfortunately, Black women are among the hardest hit and are projected to be the least able to recover from the effects of the pandemic. The experiences of inequality among Black women are different from those of white women and even Black men. Kimberlé Crenshaw (1989) argues that Black women's position as simultaneously Black and female, and many times also as poor, gives Black women a unique history and sociohistorical viewpoint. Also, the health of Black women is impaired by a multiplicity of factors, including employment, family responsibilities, education, limited cultural competencies of medical providers, and lack of health insurance. Research data on Black women are piecemeal, and only a few studies disaggregate COVID-19 outcomes by gender and race. However, we know that Black women are often at the intersection of the worst health disparities.

According to Lovoria B. Williams (2020), Black women are more likely to suffer from comorbid conditions such as asthma, obesity, hypertension, and diabetes, all of which increase their risk of contracting the virus and dying from it. There are also challenges to adequate health access for Black women that provide additional insight into disparities in COVID-19 complications. For example, Debora de Souza Santos and colleagues (2021) evaluated the racial disparities among childbearing women within a health system during the pandemic. Their data show that maternal mortality in Black women due to COVID-19 was almost two times higher than that observed for white women. Research has also revealed that Black pregnant women have a higher likelihood of being worried about their prenatal care and birth experience than white pregnant women (Gur et al. 2020). The same study found that Black women were more resilient and had a higher level of self-reliance and emotion regulation than their white counterparts.

Black women's financial well-being has been affected by the pandemic as well. Annalyn Kurtz (2021) reported from the U.S. Bureau of Labor Statistics that Latinas currently have the highest unemployment rate at 9.1 percent, followed by Black women at 8.4 percent and white women at 5.7 percent. She also reported that in December 2020, Black women and Latinas had suffered decreases in employment, but their white women counterparts had made significant gains. Compared to white workers, Black women are more likely to work outside the home in "essential" fields (Bozarth and Hanks 2020), and more likely to hold employment that has no security. According to Anu Madgavkar and colleagues (2020), Black women are more likely to be in positions that carry no guarantees, such as grocery store clerks, personal care aides, housekeepers, and medical care support workers; thus, they are disproportionately targeted for layoffs. Black women are also more likely than others to step back from their workplace and even give up their careers due to this pandemic (Weber and Fuhrmans 2020). This is due to Black women taking on more responsibility as caregivers and other demanding support roles in and out of their homes.

The additional burden of the COVID-19 pandemic places Black women at even greater risk of all forms of abuse, including physical, emotional, and financial. Before the pandemic, several researchers noted that African American women encounter significantly higher rates of intimate partner violence than the general population of women (Lee, Thompson, and Mechanic, 2002; Hamptom and Gelles 1994; Rennison and Welchans 2000). In one study, Black women experienced intimate partner violence at a rate that was 35 percent higher than that for white women (Rennison and Welchans 2000). Tricia B. Bent-Goodley (2009) affirmed that women of color are more likely to be discriminated against and less likely to obtain much-needed health services. Unfortunately, services are often limited and have historically taken a "color-blind" or one-size-fits-all approach (Gillum 2008; Thomas 2001; Taylor 2000).

Theoretical Framework

An intersectional framework seeks to explain how social and political identities such as race, gender, ethnicity, class, ability, and sexuality create conditions and experiences of discrimination or privilege (Crenshaw 1989, 1997). These interactions occur within a context of connected systems and power structures like laws, policies, governments, religious institutions, and media. While many scholars are influenced by the concept of intersectionality (Hancock 2016), Black feminist scholar Kimberlé Crenshaw developed this theory. Crenshaw's theoretical framework allows us to understand better how inequalities exist. It enables us to challenge simple comparisons, like men and women. bell hooks (1992) challenged the notion that gender was the primary factor determining women's fate. I utilize the intersectional perspective to assess those most at risk and those disproportionately affected by the COVID-19 pandemic, such as Black women and people with disabilities. Adopting an intersectional lens makes it possible for me to consider how deeply rooted social inequalities intersect for people in relation to COVID-19 and the public health and welfare system.

As the COVID-19 pandemic unfolded, so did layers of risk and barriers for individuals at the margins, especially for Black women and people with disabilities. This analysis allowed me to capture various intersecting factors to uncover how differently situated groups and populations are experiencing COVID-19. Analysis of the impacts of COVID-19 in the context of intersecting oppressions offers the potential for a better understanding of the impacts of the virus and contributes to the literature on disability studies. Intersectionality provides a framework for understanding and legitimizing the unique experiences of COVID-19 among Black women and allows me to voice my personal experience with COVID-19 as a differently abled Black woman.

Methodology

Research rarely provides a safe place for Black women to tell their truth (Houston and Davis 2002). Black feminist autoethnography does this, allowing Black women the space to read and record their unique experiences (Griffin 2012). Utilizing Black feminist autoethnography, I address the experiences of COVID-19 among Black women and people with disabilities from the perspective of a differently abled Black woman. The edited collection *Tedious Journeys: Autoethnography by Women of Color in Academe* (Robinson and Clardy 2010) inspired my use of autoethnography. The women who tell their stories in *Tedious Journeys* illuminate the experiences of women of color in predominantly white institutions.

Furthermore, Black feminist autoethnography allows me to see how COVID-19 uncovers disproportionate risk and impact based on structural inequality at the intersections of race, ethnicity, gender, ability, and class. This perspective challenges us to look at prevailing racial inequalities in COVID-19 outcomes. Ultimately, this approach offers me a place in academia to tell my experience and advocate for myself as a differently abled Black woman in a space where my voice is often ignored. The representation for Black women is more than a request. It is necessary! Through this analysis, I seek to deepen our understanding of COVID-19, inclusion, and opportunities for at-risk populations, especially disabled women of color.

A Seat at the Table?

Calling on a popular adage, Senator Elizabeth Warren (D-Mass.) said in 2019 that "if you don't have a seat at the table, you're probably on the menu" (Trudo 2019). The statement suggests that one must be present at the negotiation table to influence a decision. Therefore, an unfavorable decision is likely if one is absent. I would say, "a seat at the table is not enough if there is not enough representation." My experience as a differently abled Black woman in the academy shows me that a seat at the table does not ensure representation. Representation goes beyond a seat at the table. It is about cultivating spaces where people can speak their truth and support the reality of others. In what follows, I describe my experiences at the table.

At One End of the Table: Researcher

As I sit at the table as an insider researcher, I find myself amused at how the COVID-19 pandemic has normalized accommodations that were once denied to me as well as to others like me. The COVID-19 pandemic exposes hypocrisy over the use of disability accommodations. Consider that educators switched physical classes to online in the blink of an eye, and businesses allowed teleworking. Working from home became the new normal for many workers during the COVID-19 pandemic; most people were given accommodations without documentation. People with disabilities, myself included, have long been requesting accommodations, the same type of accommodations that quickly rolled out en masse once lockdowns began. For instance, pre-COVID-19, I fought many battles to receive accommodations that are guaranteed through the disability rights acts. I recall a graduate school situation where I requested to use my accommodations: a quiet space, oral communication, a keyboard, and double time for completing the comprehension exam. Despite my having the proper documentation, my institution chose which accommodations it was willing to provide to me. Postgraduation, I watched the news and posts on Facebook declaring that the institution I had once attended had switched classes to online and dissertation defenses and comprehensive exams to home settings.

Previously, these events were strictly face-to-face, with no exceptions for extenuating circumstances. When I did request accommodations, others often questioned the legitimacy of my needs. I remember one incident in which a professor told me that the use of accommodations would cause others to question my abilities. Ultimately, it caused me to doubt my abilities. Because of the constant questioning, I often went without my accommodations to accommodate others. Now, I often question my abilities; being treated as an imposter is even more real for me. I do not see many examples of people who look like me or share the same background; the lack of representation often makes me feel like an outsider. In the disability research space, I am not disabled enough due to my hidden conditions. Accommodations are often seen as "special treatment" or an "advantage." Disability advocate Heather Watkins made this point in a Facebook post on December 30, 2021. She pointed out that before the pandemic, many people with disabilities were prevented from attending classes and making it to their medical appointments and other events because of accessibility issues. In contrast, she noted, with events going virtual due to the pandemic, many disabled people were finally getting the opportunities to connect that we have always deserved. Once deemed complex and impossible, requests for teleconferencing and the opportunity to work remotely are *now* viewed as valuable and necessary. But many of us now only benefit because it was deemed necessary for nondisabled individuals. We remain a second thought even now. Despite the Americans with Disabilities Act of 1990 mandating accommodations, receiving accommodations is not consistent among people with disabilities (Daly and Noble 1996; Balser 2007). During the pandemic, one in five disabled workers had their requests to work at home denied (Faragher 2020), thus forcing them to choose between making a living or staying safe. The U.K. disability equality charity Scope (2020) reported that 20 percent of people with disabilities were placed in an "impossible position" during the pandemic.

Unfortunately, disadvantages such as lower education levels, lower employment rates, fewer household resources, and poor health have contributed to the exclusion of individuals with disabilities from the workplace and academia. There are data on employment, race, and disability, but there are limited data on the intersection of these disparities. Disabled people of color, especially minority women with disabilities, are often uncounted in the research, which leaves their unique issues and experiences untold.

At the Other End of the Table: Differently Abled Black Woman, "Subject"

Now, I sit at the other end of the table as the research subject. When I first became aware of the pandemic, I was concerned, but not overly concerned, because it seemed like COVID-19 only harmed white communities, or at least this is what was circulating on social media. As the virus spread, the outcomes changed, and then the news reported that Black and brown communities and people with preexisting conditions were more at risk and dying at higher rates from the virus. Anxiety and fear consumed me. While I experienced anxiety before the pandemic, it was compounded and more isolating.

For me, the pandemic brought into stark contrast the intersecting challenges of being a Black woman with multiple health conditions. I found myself fearful and worried about my health, my loved ones, my adult students, other people like me, and the support services I rely on. My anxiety was so intense that when I witnessed empty shelves in supermarkets, I experienced breathing problems, which resulted in me leaving immediately. My experiences include being challenged when I attempted to use the special shopping hours for vulnerable populations. I was stopped by an employee and told these hours are only for seniors and vulnerable people. I had to plead and explain that I am one of those vulnerable individuals; my conditions are not visible to the naked eye.

No one or nothing could ever have prepared me for this. My doctor increased my anxiety medicine dosage. I increased counseling, used the special shopping hours for vulnerable populations, and ordered food and medication online. All of these were useful but came with their own set of challenges. For example, when I ordered food or medication online, I found the system overused by the general public, which caused long waits. Obtaining prescriptions online was the biggest challenge for me. My medicine would often be delayed by as much as a week, or medications such as those for anxiety and seizures were out of stock. These are medicines I need to live. The pandemic also brought about changes to health and counseling appointments and treatment. Appointments changed to teleconferencing and Zoom sessions.

I felt overwhelmed by the system and technology, which increased my anxiety and stress. For the most part, I am somewhat tech savvy. Imagine others like me who are not so tech savvy. Every part of my life was using technology, including work, counseling, doctors' appointments, and communications with loved ones and friends. Eventually, I changed my counseling session from a Zoom session to a basic phone. I was over-Zoomed. This small change helped reduce my anxiety.

Suddenly, the world went chaotic, and institutions in North Carolina and other states switched from face-to-face classes to online classes during spring 2020. Spring break was extended an extra week at my institution to plan and put coursework online. I had four physical classes to switch over within a week. It was very stressful for my students and me because of the unknown and the uncertainty of the pandemic. Once the first semester with COVID-19 ended, it left me mentally sick for the better part of the week; I barely ate or felt like completing essential everyday tasks.

Like many others, I was left to choose between preserving my health or returning to work and making ends meet. I found myself juggling both options. As I entered a new semester, Fall 2020, I found myself again scared and in limbo about returning to face-to-face classes. COVID was still very much here. My institution gave all of us a choice to teach online, hybrid, or face-to-face. Whether to go back to work felt like an impossible decision. Suddenly, it hit me; I would need to figure out how to work and teach remotely during the pandemic. For the Fall 2020 semester, I decided to place my courses online, with some asynchronous and synchronous courses, to protect myself, my family, my students, and my colleagues. I am confident and feel very strong with teaching courses face-to-face because I can gauge whether students understand the course material; teaching online is more complicated.

Teaching entirely online during the pandemic was exhausting and challenging. My ADHD never took a break, not even for the COVID-19 pandemic. Remote work while managing ADHD made it difficult to stay focused and complete work-related tasks. I found myself washing clothes, cleaning the house, or washing dishes instead of working on tasks related to my job. To manage my ADHD, I created daily and weekly routines. I made to-do lists, assigned time to tasks, created a calm and uncluttered workspace in my home, and scheduled exercise and meditation sessions. Then the unthinkable happened. I became infected with COVID-19. I had done everything possible to protect myself and others. I placed courses online, wore a mask, washed my hands, socially distanced, and used online services to obtain my basic needs. Ironically, I likely received the infection from a face-to-face doctor's appointment, infected by my nurse, a Black woman who was also severely affected by the pandemic. She was forced to travel to care for a family member and could not quarantine when she returned because her hours had been reduced from full time to part time due to the pandemic. She also found herself at two ends of a table as both a care provider and a patient because of COVID-19.

The doctor ordered me to isolate and rest. Here I was single and living alone, which brought about another set of fears; I could be dead, maybe even decaying, and no one would know. But I had a semester to finish and grading to complete. I had to isolate myself and push through the end of the fall semester, even as I battled COVID-19. Due to breathing complications, I was hospitalized for several days. The experience at the hospital was horrible, to say the least. Due to lack of space at my nearby hospital, I was treated in a hospital in another county. And my experience with the nursing staff reminded me of how Black women are often judged. The nurse suggested that I had not followed the governor's request to refrain from holiday festivities, implying that I was now suffering from poor decision-making. Yet, I had done everything correctly. This was so degrading.

Now it is the Spring 2022 semester. My university has returned to an expectation of normalcy, despite the ongoing pandemic. Sadly, I have returned to the status quo of prepandemic days, a world overwhelmed by complex barriers to inclusion. The Centers for Disease Control and Prevention, President Biden, and my institution promote the line that the best defense against COVID-19 is to get the vaccine. What if you can't get the vaccine? Because I have multiple health conditions, my doctors do not recommend the vaccine. Everyone's opinions about vaccination differ, but it is hard to hear statements about unvaccinated people. For example, unvaccinated people are selfish and deserve to die or lose their jobs. Unfortunately, I am a part of the unvaccinated group, not by choice. So, do I deserve to die? Or do I deserve to lose my job?

As I taught during the height of the omicron outbreak, my institution had yet to develop clear or tailored policies and procedures. For example, I attempted to submit health documentation from my doctors to the disability office at my university to set up accommodation for teaching during the pandemic, only to be informed that the office was unaware of how to help me or any other faculty member with my exact needs. To clarify pandemic policies and procedures for teaching, I emailed upper management. The result was long email threads with no clear policies and procedures. Due to ableist expectations that everyone can follow mandates and unclear guidelines, these situations were extremely challenging for me. They could have similar harm for faculty or staff with health conditions. When the university was making procedures for COVID-19, where was the representation and support for faculty and staff with disabilities and health conditions? And are there any provisions for students with health problems? We must advocate for ourselves because our employers are not paying attention. They are too busy making business decisions rather than moral decisions. So, with all that said and done, I found myself at both ends of the table, a researcher at one end and the subject of the analysis at the other—the life and times of a differently abled Black woman during COVID-19.

Conclusion

Throughout the pandemic, I have sat at both ends of the table. I am simultaneously a researcher and a research subject. And this has been my testimony. The COVID-19 pandemic has completely changed our lives, and our lives may remain changed in major ways when the pandemic is over. However, we must not continue to leave behind those at the margins, those who suffer disproportionately. As we face COVID-19, we must tackle the virus through an intersectional lens. COVID-19 does not discriminate with regard to race, ethnicity, religion, age, gender, ability, socioeconomic status, or politics, but it does disproportionately cause more harm to those in vulnerable positions. Although communities may share many experiences, some important and unique differences need to be understood to effectively combat the virus. My autoethnography highlights the intersecting impacts of the COVID-19 pandemic as we consider gender, race, class, and ability, contributing to the literature on disability studies by using an intersectional approach. Bridging the Black feminist and disability field allows us to fill the literature gap between Black studies and disability studies. It also allows us to capture how social constructions of disability, gender, and Blackness shape the realities and the lived experiences for those multiply marginalized within humanity (Mobley and Bailey 2019; Chapple 2019).

There is little to no research on Black women or other minorities and how disability affects them, and there is even less literature on how COVID-19 has affected these populations. Disability is often left out of consideration when researchers analyze intersectional identities. This study brings in another level of analysis by including a population continually at the margins within intersectional theory—Black differently abled women. Utilizing an intersectional approach and autoethnographic methodology, I hope to demonstrate how this pandemic affected those at the margins, such as myself, thus advancing intersectionality theory and influencing policymaking.

References

Adler, Patricia A., and Peter Adler. 1994. "Observational Techniques." In *Handbook of Qualitative Research*, edited by Norman K. Denzin and Yvonna S. Lincoln, 377–92. Thousand Oaks, Calif.: Sage.

Balser, Deborah B. 2007. "Predictors of Workplace Accommodations for Employees with Mobility-Related Disabilities." *Administration and Society* 39 (5): 656–83.

Bell, Christopher M., ed. 2011. *Blackness and Disability: Critical Examinations and Cultural Interventions.* Münster: LIT Verlag.

Bent-Goodley, Tricia B. 2001. "Eradicating Domestic Violence in the African American Community: A Literature Review and Action Agenda." *Trauma, Violence, and Abuse* 2 (4): 316–30.

Bent-Goodley, Tricia B. 2009. "A Black Experience–Based Approach to Gender-Based Violence." *Social Work* 54 (3): 262–69.

Bozarth, Kendra, and Angela Hanks. 2020. "Structural Racism Is Exacerbating the Coronavirus Pandemic for Black People—Especially Black Women." *Ms.,* April 9, 2020. https://msmagazine.com/2020/04/09/structural-racism-is-exacerbating-the-coronavirus-pandemic-for-black-people-especially-black-women/.

Campbell, Vincent A., Jamylle A. Gilyard, Lisa Sinclair, Tom Sternberg, and June I. Kailes. 2009. "Preparing for and Responding to Pandemic Influenza: Implications for People with Disabilities." *American Journal of Public Health* 99 (S2): S294–S300.

Centers for Disease Control and Prevention. 2019. "Prevention of Coronavirus Disease 2019 (COVID-19): Discontinuation of Isolation for Persons with COVID-19 Not in Healthcare Settings (Interim Guidance)." Updated April 4, 2020. https://www.cdc.gov/coronavirus/2019-ncov/hcp/disposition-in-home-patients.html.

Centers for Disease Control and Prevention. 2021. CDC COVID Data Tracker. Accessed November 15, 2021. https://covid.cdc.gov/covid-data-tracker/#cases_casesper100klast7days.

Chapple, Reshawna L. 2019. "Toward a Theory of Black Deaf Feminism: The Quiet Invisibility of a Population." *Affilia* 34 (2): 186–98.

Crenshaw, Kimberlé. 1989. "Demarginalizing the Intersection of Race and Sex: A Black Feminist Critique of Antidiscrimination Doctrine, Feminist Theory and Antiracist Politics." *University of Chicago Legal Forum,* no. 18, 139–67.

Crenshaw, Kimberlé. 1997. "Intersectionality and Identity Politics: Learning from Violence Against Women of Color." In *Reconstructing Political Theory: Feminist Perspectives,* edited by Mary Lyndon Shanley and Uma Narayan, 178–93. State College: Pennsylvania State University Press.

Daly, Michael, and Michael Noble. 1996. "The Reach of Disability Benefits: An Examination of the Disability Living Allowance." *Journal of Social Welfare and Family Law* 18 (1): 37–51.

Dyer, Owen. 2020. "Covid-19: Black People and Other Minorities Are Hardest Hit in US." *BMJ* 369. https://doi.org/10.1136/bmj.m1483.

Faragher, Jo. 2020. "A Fifth of Disabled Workers Had Work from Home Requests Turned Down During Pandemic." *Personnel Today*, November 23, 2020. https://www.personneltoday.com/hr/a-fifth-of-disabled-workers-had -covid-work-from-home-requests-turned-down/.

Gillum, Tameka L. 2008. "Community Response and Needs of African American Female Survivors of Domestic Violence." *Journal of Interpersonal Violence* 23 (1): 39–57.

Griffin, Rachel Alicia. 2012. "I AM an Angry Black Woman: Black Feminist Autoethnography, Voice, and Resistance." *Women's Studies in Communication* 35 (2): 138–57.

Gur, Raquel E., Lauren K. White, Rebecca Waller, Ran Barzilay, Tyler M. Moore, Sara Kornfield, Wanjiku FM Njoroge et al. 2020. "The Disproportionate Burden of the COVID-19 Pandemic Among Pregnant Black Women." *Psychiatry Research* 293: article 113475. https://doi.org/10.1016/j.psychres .2020.113475.

Hamptom, Robert L., and Richard J. Gelles. 1994. "Violence Toward Black Women in a Nationally Representative Sample of Black Families." *Journal of Comparative Family Studies* 25 (1): 105–19.

Hancock, Ange-Marie. 2016. *Intersectionality: An Intellectual History*. Oxford: Oxford University Press.

hooks, bell. 1992. *Yearning: Race, Gender, and Cultural Politics*. New York: South End Press.

Houston, Marsha, and Olga Idriss Davis, eds. 2002. *Centering Ourselves: African American Feminist and Womanist Studies of Discourse*. New York: Hampton Press.

Jordan, Adrienne. 2018. "Advice for Black Women on How to Eat to Combat Heart Disease from A Black Female Cardiologist." *Essence*, August 31, 2018.

Kurtz, Annalyn, 2021. "The US Economy Lost 140,000 Jobs in December. All of Them Were Held by Women." *CNN Business*, January 8, 2021. https://edition .cnn.com/2021/01/08/economy/women-job-losses-pandemic/index.html.

Landes, Scott D., Margaret A. Turk, Margaret K. Formica, and Katherine E. McDonald. 2020. "COVID-19 Trends Among Adults with Intellectual and Developmental Disabilities (IDD) Living in Residential Group Homes in New York State Through July 10, 2020." Research Brief no. 32. Lerner Center for Public Health Promotion. September 16, 2020. https://surface.syr.edu /lerner/13.

Laurencin, Cato T., and Joanne M. Walker. 2020. "A Pandemic on a Pandemic: Racism and COVID-19 in Blacks." *Cell Systems* 11 (1): 9–10.

Lee, Roberta K., Vetta L. Sanders Thompson, and Mindy B. Mechanic. 2002. "Intimate Partner Violence and Women of Color: A Call for Innovations." *American Journal of Public Health* 92 (4): 530–34.

Lund, Emily M., Anjali J. Forber-Pratt, Catherine Wilson, and Linda R. Mona. 2020. "The COVID-19 Pandemic, Stress, and Trauma in the Disability Community: A Call to Action." *Rehabilitation Psychology* 65 (4): 313–22.

Madgavkar, Anu, Olivia White, Mekala Krishnan, Deepa Mahajan, and Xavier Azcue. 2020. "COVID-19 and Gender Equality: Countering the Regressive Effects." McKinsey Global Institute. July 15, 2020. https://www.mckinsey.com/featured-insights/future-of-work/covid-19-and-gender-equality-countering-the-regressive-effects.

Mitra, Sophie, and Douglas Kruse. 2016. "Are Workers with Disabilities More Likely to Be Displaced?" *International Journal of Human Resource Management* 27 (14): 1550–79.

Mobley, Izetta Autumn, and Moya Bailey. 2019. "Work in the Intersections: A Black Feminist Disability Framework." *Gender and Society* 33 (1): 19–40.

Okoro, Catherine A., NaTasha D. Hollis, Alissa C. Cyrus, and Shannon Griffin-Blake. 2018. "Prevalence of Disabilities and Health Care Access by Disability Status and Type Among Adults—United States, 2016." *Morbidity and Mortality Weekly Report* 67 (32): 882–87.

O'Sullivan, Tracey, and Maxime Bourgoin. 2010. "Vulnerability in an Influenza Pandemic: Looking Beyond Medical Risk." Unpublished. ResearchGate. Uploaded October 2010. https://www.researchgate.net/publication/282817477.

Petersilia, Joan R. 2001. "Crime Victims with Developmental Disabilities: A Review Essay." *Criminal Justice and Behavior* 28 (6): 655–94.

Rennison, Callie Marie, and Sarah Welchans. 2000. "Intimate Partner Violence." Bureau of Justice Statistics Special Report. May 2000. NCJ 178247.

Robinson, Cynthia Cole, and Pauline Clardy, eds. 2010. *Tedious Journeys: Autoethnography by Women of Color in Academe.* New York: Peter Lang.

Sakellariou, Dikaios, Ana Paula Serrata Malfitano, and Elena S. Rotarou. 2020. "Disability Inclusiveness of Government Responses to COVID-19 in South America: A Framework Analysis Study." *International Journal for Equity in Health* 19 (1): 1–10.

Sanchez-Hucles, Janis V. 1997. "Jeopardy not Bonus Status for African American Women in the Workforce: Why Does the Myth of Advantage Persist?" *American Journal of Community Psychology* 25 (5): 565–80.

Santos, Debora de Souza, Mariane de Oliveira Menezes, Carla Betina Andreucci, Marcos Nakamura-Pereira, Roxana Knobel, Leila Katz, Heloisa de Oliveira Salgado, Melania Maria Ramos de Amorim, and Maira L. S. Takemoto. 2021. "Disproportionate Impact of COVID-19 Among Pregnant and Postpartum Black Women in Brazil Through Structural Racism Lens." *Clinical Infectious Diseases* 72 (11): 2067–68.

Scope. 2020. "Disabled People Are Facing Unthinkable Dilemma Between Health and Wages." https://www.scope.org.uk/media/press-releases/disabled-people-back-to-work-fears/.

Sood, Lakshay, and Vanita Sood. 2021. "Being African American and Rural: A Double Jeopardy from COVID-19." *Journal of Rural Health* 37 (1): 217–21.

Taylor, Janette Y. 2000. "Sisters of the Yam: African American Women's Healing and Self-Recovery from Intimate Male Partner Violence." *Issues in Mental Health Nursing* 21 (5): 515–31.

Thomas, David A. 2001. "The Truth About Mentoring Minorities: Race Matters." *Harvard Business Review* 79 (4): 98–107.

Thompson, Vilissa. 2016. "#Disability Too White: Making the 'Good Trouble' in Advocacy." *Ramp Your Voice!* (blog). May 26, 2016. http://www.rampyourvoice.com/disabilitytoowhite-making-good-trouble-advocacy/.

Trudo, Hanna. 2019. "Elizabeth Warren Leans into 'First Female President.'" *Daily Beast*, December 11, 2019. https://www.thedailybeast.com/elizabeth-warren-leans-into-first-female-president.

Unluer, Sema. 2012. "Being an Insider Researcher While Conducting Case Study Research." *Qualitative Report* 17 (29). https://doi.org/10.46743/2160-3715/2012.1752.

Weber, Lauren, and Vanessa Fuhrmans. 2020. "How the Coronavirus Crisis Threatens to Set Back Women's Careers." *Wall Street Journal*, September 30, 2020. https://www.wsj.com/articles/how-the-coronavirus-crisis-threatens-to-set-back-womens-careers-11601438460.

Williams, Lovoria B. 2020. "COVID-19 Disparity Among Black Americans: A Call to Action for Nurse Scientists." *Research in Nursing and Health* 43 (5): 440–41.

World Health Organization. 2021. "WHO Coronavirus Disease (COVID-19) Dashboard." Accessed May 13, 2021. https://covid19.who.int/.

CHAPTER 7

Stuck Between a Rock and a Hard Place

How Government Guidance to Combat COVID-19 Disproportionately Affected U.K. Immigrant Black Women

Annet Matebwe

On March 23, 2020, the U.K. government imposed the first full national lockdown in response to the novel coronavirus, COVID-19. The slogan "Stay Home, Protect the National Health Service, Save Lives" was plastered everywhere. Up until this point, the government had been accused of lacking transparency and not sufficiently engaging with people on how to best deal with the virus (Kalogeropolous and Nielsen 2020). Ultimately, the announcement of the national lockdown was received with mixed emotions. The lockdown prohibited nonessential travel and resulted in the closure of all industries considered nonessential, such as the hospitality and beauty industries. Although the guidelines seemed to apply fairly to all individuals in the United Kingdom, this was not the case. From my position as a Black immigrant woman, the guidelines seemed more detrimental to people like me. Thus, I need to share my experience. I seek to bring the discrepancies to light, hoping that my story will influence future policies and practices.

My concerns over COVID-19 did not start when the national lockdown was imposed. They started weeks earlier. When the positive cases began to rise exponentially and disaster became imminent, I remember not being concerned about the potentially life-threatening effects of the virus. Instead, I was more concerned about my immigration status. What would happen if I tested positive? Would I be deported to Zimbabwe? These were just two of the questions that came to mind. In addition to my immigration status, I wondered how I would make money to sustain myself during the pandemic as the economy had significantly slowed. I knew that redundancy was unavoidable. As a Black woman, I had to confront my immigration and employment statuses simultaneously.

I was stressed and anxious, but I also knew that I did not have the luxury of wallowing in my emotions. I had to be resourceful and resilient because at the end of the day, I could not depend on anyone other than myself. After all, the government wouldn't be concerned about me; I am a Black immigrant woman. A long time ago, I fully realized that my well-being was hardly considered a priority.

While many U.K. citizens had the luxury of arguing over how invasive the imposed lockdown was or how more needed to be done, I could barely engage as a Black immigrant woman. I had a different set of worries to preoccupy me. It seemed that my worries had not been considered by those making the law. I was invisible but yet felt targeted in a particular way.

The government guidance was clear: all nonessential industries were closed, and the government exercised sole control over what was deemed essential and what was not. The industries deemed nonessential were those that largely employ the immigrant population. This was a huge blow for me because I worked for a small, family-run coffee shop. Eventually, the forced closures resulted in the family closing the coffee shop altogether. So, amid a pandemic, I found myself jobless. I'd be lying if I said that starting an OnlyFans account didn't cross my mind.[1] However, the prospect of my African mother's disapproval and disappointment, should she find out, was enough to eradicate that idea quickly.

Although one might argue that being unemployed during the pandemic wasn't a unique position as thousands of other people were in the same predicament, I'd beg to differ. Here's why: many immigrant workers are concentrated within the hospitality and beauty industries, both of which the government deemed nonessential during the lockdown. This meant that although the national lockdown was meant to affect people equally, immigrant workers, like myself, were, in fact, the hardest hit. This has implications for our individual economic survival and for that of our families, who are dependent on our wages.

The government's decision to close all nonessential industries affected many people. But many British citizens had options that were not available to immigrants living in the United Kingdom. As an immigrant, I did not have the luxury of being placed on the government furlough scheme, which, if I were a British citizen, would have entitled me to 80 percent of my income despite not working due to the pandemic. Furthermore, I could not apply for social security and receive public funds because this would go against my study visa conditions. So, the government guidelines effectively stripped me of my sole source of income without providing me with any recourse. This left me between a rock and a hard place.

Most people would expect me to be angry and sad about the position I found myself in but, I felt neither of those emotions. I have been an immigrant long enough to know that my predicament would move nobody. I'm also a Black woman; I have grown up being labeled as "strong," a label that has stripped me of the freedom to break down and admit that I, too, need protection and help. So, as usual, I buried my sadness and frustration.

I had no option but to look for another job, one in an industry deemed essential by the government. This limited my search to essential retail and health care. As I submitted numerous applications, I discovered interesting changes the government had made to working conditions for immigrants like myself. Prepandemic, my study visa limited me to working twenty hours a week; anything above that would be considered illegal and treated as grounds for deportation.

During the pandemic, the government withdrew the twenty-hour work limit, but it did so only for jobs within health care and the caring industry—industries that posed a high risk of contracting COVID-19. Although I was happy to have the option of working more hours, which would equal more pay, I felt uneasy about how the government was using my desperation to lure me into potentially life-threatening work.

This move by the government ensured that the United Kingdom's health-care workforce could be constantly replenished by immigrants—many of whom were desperate for work. On the one hand, it was genius because it worked. I was desperate for work and ultimately applied to various roles within the National Health Service (NHS); I was never called back for an interview, which in hindsight was a blessing. I may not have received a call back as I had no prior experience working in the health-care industry. I was forced to drastically reduce my spending and live on the little savings I had. But many other immigrant Black women in the United Kingdom have experience working in hospitals and care homes, and because they were desperate for work, they joined the NHS as part of the frontline staff against COVID-19.

However, as the number of COVID-19 deaths rose, I started noticing some worrying disparities. Many frontline NHS workers who were dying were immigrant Black, Asian, and minority ethnic (BAME) individuals. This was heavily reported on the national news (*ITV* 2020). I didn't understand why the authorities found the statistics shocking, given the fact that the government had made efforts to ensure that more immigrant workers, those BAME individuals, were recruited into the NHS as part of the frontline staff against COVID-19. The government guidelines to help fight the virus led to an overrepresentation of BAME health-care workers. This undoubtedly led to a higher percentage of BAME health-care workers dying. To me, the mathematics was simple. By closing industries that immigrant workers normally saturate, the government indirectly forced immigrants into the COVID-19 front line and ultimately their deaths.

Every new media report about a Black woman dying on the COVID-19 front line broke my heart. I often wondered whether the deceased would still have pursued a career on the front lines if they had the option to work elsewhere or had been afforded substantive government aid. I grew angry. I was mad because I knew that many Black women who died working on the front lines had continued to work to ensure that they could provide for themselves and their families. The government's guidelines made it difficult to have options—something most privileged people will fail to understand.

In the midst of this all, #BlackLivesMatter protests took center stage a few months after the national lockdown. I remember sitting with a group of white British people who lived in my apartment complex. A lady brought up the #BlackLivesMatter protests. She commented on how useless the protests were because they would result in a rise in COVID-19 infections. She stated that she didn't understand why people were protesting as there were more important things to protest about, such as lack of housing. Her comments made me livid because they made me realize that all those Black lives lost as a result of being on the COVID-19 front line did not matter to her. I am embarrassed. I did not call her out on her statements because I feared being labeled the "angry Black woman." But her statements continued to haunt me, especially because I know that she is not the only one who thinks this way. I have qualms knowing that the individuals responsible for drafting the COVID-19 guidelines may share her sentiments.

My thoughts and experiences of living as a Black immigrant woman in the United Kingdom are not earth-shattering information. But I believe mine is a story worth sharing because it highlights some of the ignored problems brought about when governments make decisions that do not account for the individuals such as me, those who are simultaneously Black, woman, and immigrant. It can't be denied that governments worldwide did not know how to best deal with COVID-19. Most governments would argue that they did the best they could in light of the circumstances. The United Kingdom's plan to combat the pandemic was drafted and thought of by a group lacking diversity or a sensibility to understand how intersecting identities oppress some. Some of the problems the guidance created could have been easily recognized had the team been more diverse and able to engage in an intersectional analysis.

Suppose a more diverse group of lawmakers had formulated the COVID-19 government guidelines. Is it likely, although not definite, that they would have made an effort to consult people on the ground? And what would that have meant for policy? Black immigrant women may have had a chance to share their concerns about the pandemic, meaning that they would also have been allowed to express their concerns about their health, instead of just about their economic and immigration status.

The impact of the proposed guidelines would have been looked at holistically, and efforts would have been made to limit the disproportionate impact on Black immigrant women. This may have resulted in special grants being offered to immigrant workers who may have lost their jobs due to the pandemic, and adequate personal protective equipment being provided to the BAME individuals who opted to take up jobs as frontline staff in the NHS. I haven't said anything particularly groundbreaking; these are all simple steps the government could have taken but failed to, largely because different voices were not afforded the chance to be heard in formulating the government guidelines to combat COVID-19.

It's the year 2021, and it is baffling that diversity and representation continue to be ignored. But, now more than ever, simple stories like mine need to be shared because, although seemingly unimportant, they shed light on the often-forgotten problems and may act as a catalyst for change.

Note

1. OnlyFans is a subscription-based social media platform where users can sell and/or purchase original content, the most common content being that of a pornographic nature.

References

ITV. 2020. "'Discrimination' on Frontline of Coronavirus Outbreak May Be Factor in Disproportionate BAME deaths Among NHS staff." May 13, 2020. https://www.itv.com/news/2020-05-13/discrimination-frontline-coronavirus-covid19-black-minority-ethnic-bame-deaths-nhs-racism.

Kalogeropolous, Antonis, and Rasmus Kleis Nielsen. 2020. "Trust in UK Government and News Media COVID-19 Information Down, Concerns over Misinformation from Government and Politicians Up." Reuters Institute. June 1, 2020. https://reutersinstitute.politics.ox.ac.uk/trust-uk-government-and-news-media-covid-19-information-down-concerns-over-misinformation.

CHAPTER 8

Black Women, Just BREATHE . . .

Personal Healing During "the 'Rona"

Angela K. Lewis-Maddox

Caring for myself is not self-indulgence, it is self-preservation, and that is an act of political warfare.

—Audre Lorde, "A Burst of Light"

During a time of immense sorrow, loss, fear, and anxiety, I found myself asking if this time alone, at home, in oneness with myself, if there was a way, I could emerge better than I was before. I set an intention, which stated, "If you are the same when this is over, you have not used this time wisely." But is it possible to utilize the time during a global pandemic to experience personal healing?

I entered the pandemic broken, hurt, and despondent. During 2019, I was dealt a series of devastating blows regarding my career. The first one was in February, the next one occurred in April, and the next in November. And finally, the most devastating blow was in January 2020, as the coronavirus made its way to the United States.[1] The arrival of the virus and the subsequent stay-at-home order in my state made me face the reality of my pain. In addition to the pain I experienced, I also struggled with protecting my family's health. In the earliest days of my state's stay-at-home order, I was almost paralyzed with anxiety, coupled with the despair of my career disappointments. Despite the frustration and anxiety, I was able to heal by utilizing various tools.

In this piece, I draw on my experiences to describe how I experienced healing during the coronavirus global pandemic.

The Reckoning

As the world faced the coronavirus, it was abundantly clear that I was in an unhealthy emotional place. I wanted to get beyond the dismal feelings that I was currently experiencing. Those feelings resulted from decisions about my career made by someone who did not think my work was worthy of recognition or advancement. As such, they did not believe I deserved career advancement, and they made decisions that obstructed my planned career trajectory. According to Zuhairah Washington and Laura Morgan Roberts (2019), a lack of career advancement and professional recognition is the norm for confident, ambitious, and determined Black women, and yet here I was, another Black woman lacking career advancement. Although I received a relatively good performance evaluation while serving as an interim, a white man with less seniority at my institution and department got the permanent position. The individual tasked with the decision-making had a historical and typically unquestioned pattern of elevating mostly white men to leadership positions. This pattern of elevating white men went unquestioned for almost seven years. I saw the pattern, a close friend was affected by the pattern, and, ultimately, the pattern affected my ability to be promoted. I ended up in therapy because my work environment became uncomfortable as a bastion of patriarchy and white privilege. I was hurt and angry. Not knowing how to cope with those emotions and not having an escape made my mental state quite fragile. Therapy alone was not helpful quick enough. Despite all the tools in my wellness kit, nothing seemed to get me over this season. At the time, I could not get it together; I had the desire to, but I simply could not do as India Arie (2002) sang: "You can fly fly fly fly / You can live or you can die / You know that life is a choice you make." I just could not shake the unsettled feelings, knowing the injustice I had suffered. I wanted to fly above what happened to me, to be at peace, but I was not. I was functioning, living day to day, doing my job, and caring for my family, but I was not mindful and present. I simply went through the motions of life.

I am a spiritual woman. I pride myself on being raised in the church, attending church regularly, and reading my Bible. My spiritual upbringing kept me tinkering on the edge of chaos, never letting me fall. The edge for me was giving up on my career, my job, and just not giving a damn. On those days when it all felt overwhelming, my relationship with God served as my foundation. Kurt Carr (1999) captures my feelings best: "Depression weighed me down / But God held me close / So I wouldn't let go." I was not suicidal, but I was despondent. I was also deeply hurt, angry, and resentful that an individual with a pattern of excluding women and people from underrepresented groups from leadership positions could be and would be solely responsible for making personnel decisions unchecked.

And then, COVID-19 shows up. Within seven days after I received the most hurtful news regarding my career, the United States reported its first coronavirus case (Muccari, Chow, and Murphy 2021). Within thirty days, the United States declared the virus a health emergency, reported the first person-to-person spread, and recorded its first death. Within forty-five days, the virus made its way with full force to the United States. While dealing with the chaos with my career, I was now faced with the coronavirus pandemic.

By the beginning of March, eleven states had reported cases. By the ninth of March, thirty-seven states had confirmed cases (Su, Secon, and Kiersz 2020). It felt as if I was being engulfed and enclosed, almost suffocating, as people with COVID-19 infections got closer and closer to my state. By March 11, most states had cases, and there were several COVID-19-related deaths reported in the United States. Surprisingly, despite the spread of the virus across the country, my child's school was still in session. Daily, the map of COVID-19 spread showed me how the infections were creeping closer and closer to where we lived. At this point, it became my responsibility to protect my family, to do everything I could to maintain their safety. To be proactive, my son's father and I discussed his school attendance. We decided to email his principal on Wednesday, March 11, at 8:48 p.m. The email asked for information regarding the system's plans to keep children safe in the face of the quickly spreading virus.

We received a response the next day, March 12, around 2:00 p.m. By this point, every state connected to our state had coronavirus cases (Gamio et al. 2020). We were dissatisfied with the response, and we did not send our child to school the following day.[2] We anticipated that his school would be closed; to our surprise, it remained open. I remember awakening to the news that the school was open. The news almost took me to a place of deep anxiety as I worried about how the school would respond should we decide to keep our son out of school indefinitely. I thought: would they view this situation as truancy, and if so, what would be the consequences? In hindsight, maybe contemplating the what-ifs in the context of deep uncertainty was not the wisest thing to do. I am grateful for his father's clear perspective; he encouraged me to take things day by day. Over the weekend, on March 14, our state had its first case of the coronavirus, and the governor issued a proclamation that closed schools in the state.

One crisis averted. The following week, I struggled as our family came to grips with the fact that my husband was an essential worker. As we learned more about the virus, unsurprisingly, we learned there were disparities in diagnosis, treatment, and death rates between Black and white people. My husband and I were both in high-risk categories for complications from the virus. Social distancing and mask usage were strategies to reduce its spread. But as my husband was an essential worker, his employer was not subject to COVID-19 orders. In the early days of the virus's arrival in my state, my husband's employer did not mandate mask usage or require social distancing. My husband's position placed him within six feet of individuals daily, which sent me deeper into despair.

Once the stay-at-home orders were in place in my state, in early April, I was forced to be still with the anguish of the past year's events and the seeming inability to protect my family. I was not prepared for the stillness. I was so accustomed to being busy that being still was foreign to me. There was nowhere to go. I could no longer rely on my daily routine, of my husband going to work, of me taking my child to school and going to the gym. I felt like there was nothing to do if I was not performing my daily routine, a routine that saved me from myself. The monotony of life's daily, weekly, monthly, and yearly routines saved me from the reality of whatever I was avoiding. I stayed so busy that I did not have to recognize the hurt, pain, or despair. If I did not recognize the pain, I certainly could not deal with it. Not dealing with it meant I was not going to heal from it. Once I was forced to be still, I knew I had a choice to make.

The Choice

With the career challenges I faced alongside the pandemic, my mental state was fragile, and I found myself in a difficult place. I knew I had to do something. I did not want to sink deeper into the abyss. Although I took responsibility for my response to the events, I would not take responsibility for the injustices. I am sure that my race and gender contributed to the situation at my job. Intersectionality provides a framework for examining the relationship among race, gender, and class (Jordan-Zachary 2007). It "denotes the various ways in which race and gender interact to shape the multiple dimensions of Black women's employment experiences" (Crenshaw 1989, 139). It also provides a politics of survival for Black women. It considers that Black women are a particular class when it comes to oppression. How do Black women who are faced with oppression of race, gender, and class face it and overcome it? How could I overcome what happened to my career? What could I do to be whole? Once things shut down, I knew I needed to do something, and I could use this time to heal. Yet, I did not have a plan. All I knew was that I needed to be restored. I needed to get it together. However, the idea of simply getting it together is troubling, considering the systems of oppression under which Black people, particularly Black women, exist.

Getting it together meant I was able to function and thrive. Yet, it was also important for me to acknowledge the systemic challenges I face as a Black woman. For example, Melissa Wood Bartholomew, Abril N. Harris, and Dale Dagar Maglalang (2018, 86) state that "the blatant disregard for Black women's health has fostered egregious health disparities." Black women are at a higher risk for death or severe complications from various illnesses and conditions, including maternal/infant mortality, cardiovascular disease, and cancer. Black women also have a higher incidence of major depressive disorder than men.

Moreover, racism is a determinant of poor health in the Black community (Williams and Mohammed 2013). Knowing the injustices I face and the disparities in health outcomes for me as a Black woman, I chose to get myself together and care for myself, so that I would be better for my family and me. Thus, I adopted the mantra of many Black women before me and accepted the notion that caring for self is an act of political warfare (Lorde [1988] 2017, 130). In fact, on April 15, 2020, I placed this statement on my social media page: "If you are the same when this is over, you have not used this time wisely." I set an intention that I would practice radical self-care and healing to overcome these challenges I faced.

Restoration

I could not continue to carry the hurt from the year's events. My common coping mechanisms were not enough to get me over these obstacles. I needed to be transparent and vulnerable to let those in my inner circle know what I was experiencing and how I felt. I had to do something different to let go of the baggage, of all the hurts, disappointments, and fear. So, I did as Erykah Badu (1998) sang, "So oh, oh, oh, if you start *breathin'* babe / You won't believe it, it feels so much better, so much better baby / Bag lady, let it go let it go let it go let it go oh."

Could simply breathing be part of my healing? I am a mindfulness practitioner, meditating daily, sometimes multiple times a day. But like all the other tools in my arsenal, it was not the magic wand to heal me. Later, however, I found a way to restore my health and wholeness and to BREATHE. In *Black Women's Mental Health: Balancing Strength and Vulnerability*, Stephanie Y. Evans, Kanika Bell, and Nsenga K. Burton (2017, 4) contend that

> The modern Black woman just wants to breathe . . .
>
> get some air . . release . . .
>
> refresh and feel anew . . .
>
> love . . . and be loved . . .
>
> and she does not want to be made to feel guilty about it.

They created BREATHE, an interdisciplinary model that encompasses a set of principles to find healing and wellness for Black women. The model embraces Black women's strength and vulnerability while at the same time honoring activist traditions by talking back to oppressive forces. The model, which they hope will serve as a framework to train mental health professionals in their care for Black women, provided me with a healing framework. The model is an acronym that is defined and explained below:

B — Balance

R — Reflection

E — Energy

A — Association

T — Transparency

H — Healing

E — Empowerment

Balance refers to the idea that Black women juggle multiple identities and responsibilities. These identities and responsibilities often lead to our demise because there is so much to do. As a result, we may not always have time to practice self-care. To have balance means prioritizing our commitments so that self-care is not the last item on our long list of things to do. The model posits that for Black women to attain wellness, there must be a repositioning of commitments to manage our priorities while also practicing self-care.

Reflection is reviewing priorities and decisions. Meditation and breathing techniques can assist in reflection, which may help us shed patterns, practices, and thoughts that no longer serve any positive and healthy purpose. Reflection, in this model, is not a means of self-degradation but one of reconnection and adjustments. As part of that reflection, Stephanie Y. Evans (2015) proposes writing our stories to heal trauma. Writing allows Black women to shift narratives and reclaim ownership in our stories (Stevenson et al. 2020).

Energy deals with goal setting and affirmations. Black women may find it challenging to stay motivated in a world that consistently devalues their achievements and talents. We often feel like Fannie Lou Hamer, who, in her struggle for voting rights, stated she was sick and tired of being sick and tired. Sometimes it is difficult to find the strength or motivation to keep going. Thus, it is critical to set small, manageable goals that lead to larger goals. As we meet goals, we celebrate. Practicing affirmations also assists with shifting our energy into a more positive space.

Association speaks to the importance of Black women creating and maintaining social networks that promote, affirm, and encourage wellness. Black women build associations through sister circles, which may serve as interventions in mental health challenges. Having sister friends to share challenges and triumphs is instrumental in overcoming mental health challenges. These sister circles are safe spaces for Black women to be open about vulnerabilities, be heard, share stories, and recover from trauma. Safe spaces are Black feminist–centered spaces that place African American history and culture at the center of the lives of Black women. They are spaces where Black women can sort out struggles from the constraints of racism, sexism, classism, and heterosexism to discover wholeness, without any concern that they will experience oppression. In short, safe spaces for Black women are only for Black women (Jones 2015).

Transparency entails avoiding silence about traumatic experiences while rejecting the social stigma surrounding mental health. Although we are resilient as Black women, we must embrace our vulnerabilities by sharing our trauma, which is part of our healing. This transparency should only occur in safe spaces so we can clearly articulate our needs without fear or judgment.

Healing involves searching for ways to assist in wellness in self and others. Health cannot occur without healing. Black women are healing from centuries of trauma subjected on them by oppressive systems. Thus, we must focus on creating a culture of wellness for ourselves and our community.

Empowerment entails reclaiming authority over our own lives and our well-being. As Black women, we must decide who we are and what we will do despite stereotypes and culture.

To BREATHE is to heal. To BREATHE is to be whole. To BREATHE is to get it together in a healthy way. To BREATHE is to let it go. To BREATHE is to hold on to things that help you feel whole. I was able to utilize the BREATHE model to just BREATHE. Facebook helped

me find my sister circle during COVID-19, thereby giving me space
to experience healing and restoration. In the sections that follow, various aspects of my healing exemplify how Black women can use the
BREATHE model to restore their mind, body, and spirit to wholeness.

BREATHING Through COVID

When we think of social media today, Facebook is one of various platforms people are accustomed to using. My process of healing began
with the use of Facebook during the lockdown. Joy Harden Bradford
(2017, 81) states that Facebook allows Black women to connect around
a common interest and support one another through community. She
goes on to state that Facebook has served as communities and virtual
"support groups, or sister circles" that "have long been proven effective in assisting Black women." In short, she says, "for many Black
women," Facebook has "indeed become a system of sister circles."
Over the past few years, I have been particularly interested in social
media's more positive aspects, mainly utilizing the groups' feature on
Facebook.

Balance, Reflection, and Shifting Energy
During the initial stages of the quarantine in the United States, I
utilized social media to connect with others in two virtual support
groups. The first was a community of people who follow the acclaimed
author, speaker, coach, and television personality Iyanla Vanzant. As
a spiritual teacher, Vanzant broadcast a daily "antiviral" message on
Facebook that became routine for me during COVID-19. The messages began by merely concentrating on the breath, breathing quietly,
in stillness. Vanzant met with the community in practice for fifty days.
Her messages included meditation sessions, inspirational readings,
and things to do for the day, such as watching a movie, doing arts
and crafts with your children, or organizing and arranging different

rooms in your home. During the quarantine, I established a daily routine where I awakened to meditate in community with others across the globe. This practice helped because we were all in the same situation, dealing with the pandemic and seeking peace and balance in our minds. For that moment, we were taking breaths in unison, all bound by an invisible enemy, quarantined inside our homes to protect ourselves and others. Knowing I wanted to change and heal from the year's events, I chose to shift my energy, setting intentions to change lanes in my career; thus, I could reflect on past choices. Before the pandemic, I was on a fast track toward leadership within higher education. My healing process placed me on a different path and led me to explore other career paths. I also broadened my wellness tool kit by including inspirational texts and different breathing techniques such as pranayama, which is mind balancing (Akthar 2006). These new techniques taught me how to breathe in such a way as to clear energy from my body and to utilize affirmations during my breathing, producing balance and calm.

I was also part of a Facebook group of professional women who had a weekly practice called Friday wins, which I continue to practice. On Fridays, we exercised our gratitude muscles by sharing our list of weekly things or experiences that we found ourselves grateful for. This practice forced me to look for the good things in life instead of focusing on COVID's genuine threat or the elements or moments of my career that had gone "wrong." Also, the group had monthly focused themes. With these themes, I was able to reflect. This group also provided me with a triad of trusted individuals where I could form associations. They listened and provided feedback in a safe space. One triad meeting encouraged me to view how my thoughts and feelings influence my actions. Notwithstanding the deep pain that societal norms of injustice caused me, I learned that it was possible to shift energy and celebrate my wins, no matter how small they were.

Association, Transparency, Healing, and, Empowerment

Joy Harden Bradford (2017) notes that Facebook has become a system of sister circles. The existence of sister circles and use of social media for building association were particularly crucial during COVID-19. Social media became a means to connect during the pandemic. My most important connection was with a group of Black women in higher education.

The online group shared an invitation to participate in a writing community during the pandemic. I thought this was an excellent opportunity to get my career back on track while writing in community. What struck me about the invitation was the description of our writing time as sacred, a notion I had never considered. Despite my twenty years in the academy, writing was just part of the job; writing was not sacred to me. It was what I must do to keep my job. Most of my job was almost always performed in isolation.

I did not know what to expect. We were to meet for six weeks for two hours with breaks. The organizers asked us to commit to being present for three weeks to build community. I signed up, received the invitation, and readied myself. Memorial Day was our first day. The environment was accepting, open, inviting, understanding, and all I had longed for in my twenty-year career. On the screen, more than twenty women in higher education were present at the same time. It was exuberant.

We were all experiencing isolation from COVID. And as Black women in higher education, we were all tied to this one destiny of writing as a career. Each day we met in community with an incantation. Afterward, we would write together in our sister circle. This sister circle completed the elements in the BREATHE model for me during COVID. It was my association, transparency, healing, and empowerment. Six weeks stretched to twelve. For twelve weeks, this was our routine. We wrote. We shared. We meditated. We prayed. We cried. We healed. We were transparent. We worked in community. Despite the isolation and separation of the pandemic, virtual spaces helped create support networks. Being in community with other Black women in higher education and meditating in community through Facebook completed a necessary element of my healing process.

My time with this writing group was amazing. Black women have so much joy, pride, and resilience. Through my sister circles, I discovered that I could simply BREATHE. I can "get some air . . . release . . . refresh and feel anew . . . love . . . and be loved" and not feel guilty about it (Evans, Bell, and Burton 2017, 4). They helped me put the BREATHE model into full practice by allowing me to be vulnerable in a safe space, reflecting on my career goals, and exploring other ways to positively affect the world through my writing.

What I thought was the end of something, my career, became a beautiful beginning. I do not know how; it just did. Could it be that I allowed it to happen? That, as Lauryn Hill (1998) sang in "When It Hurts So Bad," "And what you need ironically. / Will turn out what you want to be / If you just let it (if you just let it)." Even as I write this chapter, I continue to work in community with my social media sister circle. The feelings of community and belonging were so profound that we could not bear to see the group end.

Conclusion

An integral part of my thriving in life and my career is to be in community. The reflection time during the pandemic helped me realize that I needed community and that community was already there for me; I just had to let it. We all have sister circles, whether family, friends, sorority sisters, or church affiliations. We freely have access to communities that uplift and support us. Although I utilized Facebook to navigate life during the pandemic, I am conscious of how interlocking systems of oppression operate to place me in despair. In honor of our ancestors, I call these systems out, and I resist them. I also fight back by practicing self-care. I chose to form sister circles utilizing social media to help me BREATHE. Through the BREATHE model, I was able to balance, reflect, shift energy from feelings of hopelessness to hope, utilize social media to form associations so that I could heal, and consciously place myself on a path of empowerment. Black women, just BREATHE.

Notes

1. The coronavirus causes a disease the World Health Organization named COVID-19, an acronym for coronavirus disease 2019. People also commonly use "the 'Rona" to refer to the virus. This chapter utilizes all three names—coronavirus, COVID-19, and the 'Rona—interchangeably.
2. The school's response to our email, verbatim, was: "Thank you for your thoughtful questions and concerns. Our school and district have a plan in place. The district will be sending out more detailed information this evening. Thank you." Later that day, the district provided a longer email indicating that it was going over safety guidelines, was following the state as new information became available, and had an e-learning plan in place should it become necessary.

References

Akthar, Shameem. 2006. "Pranayama to the Rescue." *India Abroad*, November 24, 2006.

Arie, India. 2002. "Get It Together." By India Arie, Andrew Ramsey, Shannon Sanders, Dana Johnson, and Mel Johnson. *Voyage to India*. Motown, 440 064 755-2. CD.

Badu, Erykah. 1998. "Bag Lady." By Erykah Badu and André Young. *Mama's Gun*. Motown, 012 153 259-2. CD.

Bartholomew, Melissa Wood, Abril N. Harris, and Dale Dagar Maglalang. 2018. "A Call to Healing: Black Lives Matter Movement as a Framework for Addressing the Health and Wellness of Black Women." *Community Psychology in Global Perspective* 4 (2): 85–100.

Carr, Kurt. 1999. "I Almost Let Go." By Kurt Carr. *Awesome Wonder*. Gospo Centric Records, 606949034221. CD.

Crenshaw, Kimberlé. 1989. "Demarginalizing the Intersection of Race and Sex: A Black Feminist Critique of Antidiscrimination Doctrine, Feminist Theory, and Antiracist Politics." *University of Chicago Legal Forum*, no. 18, 139–67.

Evans, Stephanie Y. 2015. "Healing Power in Black Women's Writing: Resources for Poetry Therapy." *Journal of Poetry Therapy* 28 (3): 165–78.

Evans, Stephanie Y., Kanika Bell, and Nsenga K. Burton. 2017. *Black Women's Mental Health: Balancing Strength and Vulnerability*. Albany: State University of New York Press.

Gamio, Lazaro, Mitch Smith, Karen Yourish, and Sarah Almukhtar. 2020. "Watch How the Coronavirus Spread Across the United States." *New York Times*, March 21, 2020.

Harden Bradford, Joy. 2017. "Selfies, Subtweets, and Suicide: Social Media as a Mediator and Agitator of Mental Health for Black Women." In *Black Women's Mental Health: Balancing Strength and Vulnerability*, edited by Stephanie Y. Evans, Kanika Bell, and Nsenga K. Burton, 75–84. Albany: State University of New York Press.

Hill, Lauryn. 1998. "When It Hurts So Bad." By Lauryn Hill. *The Miseducation of Lauryn Hill*. Ruffhouse Records, CK 69035. CD.

Jones, Lani V. 2015. "Black Feminisms: Renewing Sacred Healing Spaces." *Affilia* 30 (2): 246–52.

Jordan-Zachery, Julia S. 2007. "Am I a Black Woman or a Woman Who Is Black? A Few Thoughts on the Meaning of Intersectionality." *Politics and Gender* 3 (2): 254–63.

Lorde, Audre. (1988) 2017. *A Burst of Light and Other Essays*. Mineola, N.Y.: Ixia Press.

Muccari, Robin, Denise Chow, and Joe Murphy. 2021. "Coronavirus Timeline: Tracking the Critical Moments of Covid-19." *NBC News*, January 1, 2021.

Stevenson, Brea, Sonja Andrews, NaTasha Robinson, and Donielle Pace. 2020. "Bridging the Academy and the Community, One Breath at a Time: The Healing Power of Africana Women's Studies." In *Persistence Is Resistance: Celebrating 50 Years of Gender, Women and Sexuality Studies*, edited by Julie Shayne. Seattle: University of Washington Pressbooks. Online book. https://uw.pressbooks.pub/happy50thws/.

Su, Ruobing, Holly Secon, and Andy Kiersz. 2020. "An Animated Map Shows How the Coronavirus Spread Through the US, State by State, Since the First Confirmed Case in January." *Business Insider*, April 21, 2020.

Washington, Zuhairah, and Laura Morgan Roberts. 2019. "Women of Color Get Less Support at Work: Here's How Managers Can Change That." *Harvard Business Review*, March 4, 2019.

Williams, David R., and Selina A. Mohammed. 2013. "Racism and Health I: Pathways and Scientific Evidence." *American Behavioral Scientist* 57 (8): 1152–73.

CHAPTER 9

Reflections on COVID from a Ten-Year-Old Black Queen

Elizabeth Peart

When I first tested positive for COVID-19, I felt embarrassed that my whole class had to quarantine, and it was because of me. I also felt frustrated that after all my family and I had been through and what we had done not to get it, that was actually when I had it. 😤 And I felt scared that I had the virus and that it would affect me badly. I thought to myself, "I will have to prepare for days of extreme headaches and weakness." 😟 Good thing it wasn't that bad, and now I'm fine; I don't have COVID anymore!

At first, I was nervous about going back to school. I thought my friends would be mad at me because I was the reason we had to go virtual. 😕 My friend Eliza sent me a card saying, "Get well soon!" and how there was nothing to be afraid of going back to school because my friends aren't mad at me! I thought that was really sweet. It made me more confident to go to school knowing my friends were fine and still healthy and that we DON'T have to be virtual again. Now I find it funny that I was concerned about what other people (my friends) would think about me, knowing I had COVID. So, I think I was more concerned that they would think of me as "contagious" and "diseased," like COVID was a long-lasting, permanent sickness.

My thoughts about me and COVID reminded me of a story I read called *Ghosts* by Raina Telgemeier. In one scene, Cat, one of the main characters, makes new friends in her new town. Anyway, she didn't want to tell her new friends about her little sister, Maya, because she thought they would ask many questions about her. Her little sister had a lung problem that made it difficult for her to run and play. Cat didn't want them to know this about her sister because she would have to explain and answer questions like "Ooh! WhAt'S sHe LiKe?!" and "OmG i WaNnA sEe HeR!!" She didn't want Maya to be embarrassed because she would feel different, odd, like she was the only one who had it, and she would feel alone. This is how I felt about going back to school after COVID-19: I was afraid that my friends would treat me like I was odd and different; I felt like I was forever contagious. To summarize, even though I knew it was only gonna be temporary, it felt permanent, considering the way I thought my friends would treat me.

My experience with COVID and feeling different reminds me of a book we were reading in class, *Lions of Little Rock* by Kristin Levine. In that book, white kids didn't want to get close to Black kids; they treated Black people how present-day people are treating COVID-19. People don't want to go anywhere near someone who has COVID—just for their safety. But, they did the same to Black people. They didn't want to look at them or be near them. And just like the story of Ruby Bridges, everyone made their children leave that school because they thought Ruby was so-called "toxic."

I once heard a Black woman on the news talking about COVID-19 and racism, and she sounded very angry. It was about the #Black-LivesMatter protests. Around that time, COVID was spreading badly, and many people had gotten it. And the news was also saying that worldwide #BlackLivesMatter protests were going on, and people were being really serious about #BlackLivesMatter. The woman was saying a few things, but the last thing she said caught my ear. She said, "There are two viruses. And we need to fight the bigger one"—or something like that.

COVID frustrates me a lot: It keeps us apart from one another, which makes it lonely for a few people, including me. It caused us to stay at home for almost six or seven months. It makes us have to wear masks all the time, and it can be a health hazard to some because some people might have trouble breathing, or if you have a baby, they can't wear masks because of how young they are. But I agree that racism is the REAL virus because racism has been around way longer than coronavirus has, and we've been trying to stop it for ages now. It's been around ever since the Pilgrims "founded" the United States.

In school, we are reading *Brown Girl Dreaming* by Jaqueline Woodson. The book talks about Jaqueline growing up, being segregated, and going to protests. For my homework, my teacher assigned us reflection questions, and one of the questions was to make up a three-sentence poem about what's going on with the book. Here is what I wrote:

We look outside
On Civil Rights they ride
not resting until justice is on our side

Peace out, homies!

CHAPTER 10

Semhle, Sbwl

Where Black Women Can Meet Grief During and Beyond a Pandemic

Mbali Mazibuko

Under the conditions of the COVID-19 pandemic and the subsequent lockdown measures implemented across the globe, but in South Africa in particular, a plethora of literature surrounding the health and socioeconomic implications of the virus has been written and widely disseminated.[1] Most notably and alarmingly, an increase in spectacular forms of violence such as gender-based violence and femicide has been brought to mainstream attention and public discourse (Ramafoko 2020). Every day in South Africa, there are reports of women and children having been raped and brutally murdered by their partners and other family members with whom they were locked down. The current South African government has developed several strategies to address the surge in violence, such as a national gender-based violence hotline and, most recently, the Gender-Based Violence and Femicide Response Fund (Brown-Luthando 2020; South African Government News Agency 2021). Every day we are also bombarded with campaigns that depict broken and battered women, as well as signages marked with the words "Real men don't rape." We could unpack the shortcomings of such strategies and campaigns, but I do not wish to get into those here. Instead, I focus on the other ways we have experienced COVID-19, ways that do not simply perpetuate a narrative of women as victims.

We seldom delve into the effect of economies of grief that are attached to gender-based violence or other systemic inequities such as poverty and poor service delivery. As I have argued elsewhere, the grief of the international community in the wake of COVID-19, which presents itself as new simply because it has disrupted privileged lives, is not new to some of us occupying disenfranchised positionalities (Mazibuko 2020). Being Black and a woman from the Global South presents unique historical and contemporary systemic challenges rooted in the imperialist agenda. Of course, while I am a Black South African woman, I am also middle class and university educated, which places me in a far more privileged position than most poor Black women in South Africa. Therefore, it is important to recognize that it is from that position that I write and speak. I connect primarily with the women I refer to and reference in my reflection here from that position.

Our experiences as Black women are not homogenous, but they remain connected and essentialized by the imperialist and hetero-patriarchal world we all inhabit. The African feminist perspective I ground this research in also emphasizes the heterogeneity of African women on the continent and across the Diaspora. And perhaps middle-class sensibilities permit me to give this reflection that insists on world-making perspectives as a break from the grief given unfairly and violently to Black women.

We are seldom given an opportunity or room to archive the intersectional and feminist approaches to COVID-19 that consider race and gender in ways that also show the cocreative and re-creative capacities of Black women. Here, from a feminist standpoint, I ask: when grief sits on our chest, as an almost perpetual condition of being a Black woman, is there room for us to move alongside it in modes of joy and community? Violence and grief are not the only languages we know; neither should they be the single narrative shoved down our throats in every seminar, advert, or billboard that engages the nexus of COVID-19, race, and gender. I argue that violence and grief do not cease to exist when Black women choose to sit in joy and community with one another. Parallel to the violence and grief is a re-creative and celebratory world-making project that lends itself to feminist imaginaries. I engage some of the eclectic and, at times, seemingly contradictory ways that Black women, in particular, have shown up for themselves—ourselves—in modes of self-care and agency. Instagram and Twitter have been particularly instrumental in archiving some of these practices, especially considering the now compulsory virtual ways of connection and communication directly resulting from the pandemic.

I reflect on the phrases *semhle* and *sbwl* and specifically focus on their appearance and circulation on Black Twitter and Instagram. I report on how Black women have applied these phrases, in virtual communities, as a means of holding us together in celebration and joy. I reference the Don't Rush Challenge and the Book Covers as Outfits Challenge as they emerged on social media under the hard lockdown in South Africa, linking these challenges to the Xhosa phrase *semhle*. From there, I consider the food practices employed under the hard lockdown in South Africa, focusing on the labor of cooking as home work and the act of sharing recipes as community-building praxis. I link these food practices to the Xhosa term *sbwl* as I consider how the food practices of these women can come from autonomous and joyful places and not simply occur as a product of patriarchal oppression. The responses to the Don't Rush Challenge and the Book Covers as Outfits Challenge, and the food practices as they have been shared and curated on Black Twitter and Instagram, inspire a reading of the life force of digital lifeworlds and women's self-expression and community building within them.

Mapping Virtual Architectures and Digital Lifeworlds

While some features of social media platforms such as Instagram, TikTok, and Twitter overlap, I find it essential to draw out the architecture of these spaces and the role each plays in women's community-

building processes. TikTok and Instagram are apps designed for curating body performance through the audiovisual. Twitter allows
for social media activity known as microblogging and is designed
mainly as a space for text and discourse through posts of 280 characters known as tweets (Malik, Heyman-Schrum, and Johri 2019). Often, if not always, content posted on Instagram and TikTok is shared
on Twitter, where active engagement is therefore encouraged. Black
Twitter is the virtual space of engagement that is coded and guided
by those of us connected by similar Black contexts and cultural experiences (McDonald 2014). Therefore, Black Twitter is a social media
subculture. André Brock Jr. (2020:79–124) defines Black Twitter as
an online gathering of Twitter users who identify as Black and use
the platform's features to perform Black discourse and forge familiar-
ity, connection, and commonplace. Black Twitter emerges as a digital
space for a Black linguistic, iconographic, historical, and provocative
local and global community. Before Black Twitter was recognized
as a social media cultural community, as Meredith D. Clark (2018)
argues, we were simply "Black on Twitter." Black Twitter is an intentional space where Black people discourse on things that concern us
and our communities. Black Twitter, therefore, constitutes a virtual
lifeworld. It is also where the social media Don't Rush Challenge and
Book Covers as Outfits Challenge appear as Diasporic Black cultural
moments. Therefore, within the lifeworld of Black Twitter, I reflect
on these two creative expressions during the COVID-19 pandemic. It
is also within the context of Black Twitter that I extrapolate African
women's food practices and community building during the lockdown in South Africa.

However, in my reference to Black Twitter, I also mean a community that includes diverse and intersecting axes of difference, and
one that incorporates women's voices, experiences, and perspectives.
Such lifeworlds require our attention as they present an opportunity
to destabilize systemic inequalities, of which gender-based discrim-

ination and women's erasure are part and parcel. I, therefore, offer a reading of Black women's participation in social media in the context of COVID-19 that shows our agentic and community-building capacities.

Communities and Connections Through Social Media

Given the time-space compression further exasperated by COVID-19 and the subsequent calls to stay home and social distance, social media spaces such as Instagram and Twitter have been more widely used and relied on as a source of connection and communication.

Guobin Yang and Rosemary Clark (2015) argue that social media removes the barriers required for connecting with others and for developing networks and communities of care, compassion, and change. Similarly, Sarah Helen Chiumbu and Dina Ligaga (2013) assert that information and communications technology enables the construction of new publics. Hester Baer (2016, 18) suggests that digital platforms have the potential to "broadly disseminate feminist ideas, shaping new modes of discourse about gender and sexism, connecting to different constituencies, and allowing different modes of protest to emerge."

While I am not focused on obvious forms of digital protest exhibited by hashtag movements like those petitioning against sexual violence (such as the #MeToo movement on Twitter), I do show how African women's self-expression in digital lifeworlds frustrates hegemonic patriarchal views of what women can and cannot do and how we should and should not look. Francesca Sobande and Krys Osei (2020) have argued that media and aesthetic activity can be regenerative for Black women. By regenerative, they refer to the potential for Black women to reimagine life and politics by engaging in media cultures for joy and pleasure. The work of Patricia T. Clough (2008) also suggests that through biotechnologies, of which social media is a part, people's potentialities can be extended, and bodies made open to more productive effects. By articulating ourselves online, we are mediated in ways beyond the neurological and biological aspects of the body, therefore opening to energy. This allows us to experience unintended effects such as joy, wherein our engagement in media activity opens up our senses to economies other than the ones we are conscious of and in control of. As I will show in the examples in this chapter, we don't anticipate that our virtual lives may forge connections and feelings of joy.

Jyoti Ahlawat (2020) postulates that women's use of social media during the COVID-19 pandemic has been especially re-creative and a bridge to sisterhood. She argues that online media has made possible a spirit of solidarity that has already been seen through digital feminist activism but that now takes on a slightly varied character. COVID-19, according to her observation, inspired women to not only share their thoughts but to collectively participate in book challenges, fashion challenges, and cooking challenges. "Sharing and collective consciousness (again) became the new normal" for women on social media.

Semhle! Black Women's Beauty and Fashion Styling in Two Social Media Challenges

I focus on the collective nature of the Xhosa phrase *semhle* as it appears in two social media challenges, the Don't Rush Challenge and the Book Covers as Outfits Challenge. I cite these cultural moments as examples of African women's way of practicing self-expression and joy through social media. Like Francesca Sobande and Krys Osei (2020), I am inspired to think about Black women's aesthetic cultures and engagement with popular media culture as sites for joy and critical resistance.

The Xhosa term *semhle* is not new and certainly did not emerge in the context of COVID-19 and the South African lockdown. However, increased mainstream use of the term grew under lockdown level 5, which ran from March 26 to April 30, 2020, and level 4, which followed, from May 1 to 31, 2020. Both lockdown levels were considered to be a hard lockdown that restricted our movements to our homes. While I cannot show all the responses to iconographic content on Twitter and Instagram here due to practical and ethical research issues,[2] I draw on some examples to demonstrate the proliferation of the term. It is important to note that it is not only Black women who use semhle as a matter of complimenting and recognizing other Black women or people in general, for that matter. Black men have also adopted the term, but this, of course, has a very different (and often heterosexual) orientation that leans toward the hypersexualization of Black women. I do not give Black men's use of semhle attention here. I intend to show how Black women code and form our own practices of care and recognition and form communities of our own. When we say semhle, what we are really saying is "I see you," and what a long overdue, important thing it is to see Black women and to see ourselves.

Semhle! Responses to the Don't Rush Challenge

Beginning in March 2020, a social media phenomenon most popular among young Black women social media users, mainly TikTok and Instagram users, dominated most of our feeds. Called the Don't Rush Challenge, it was animated through a hashtag (#DontRushChallenge), which functioned as both a stitch and a way of centralizing and archiving discourse. In likening the hashtag to a stitch, I am inspired by Zukolwenkosi Zikalala's unpublished thesis titled "Black Queers Must Play" (2016), where he thinks through the stitch as a political and cultural thread that patches and weaves together communities, experiences, and lifeworlds. Through hashtags on Twitter, discourses, moments, and news become a trend and spread across space and time.

Moving from the United States, the Don't Rush Challenge soon became our own in South Africa.

Some popular media culture news outlets, such as *Teen Vogue* (Isama 2020), cite U.K. college student Toluwase Asolo and seven of her friends as the cultural leaders of the challenge. Asolo used British rap duo Young T and Bugsey's song "Don't Rush" as the background music for a video that she posted to TikTok. In the video, Asolo captures herself in the first scene in a sleeping robe and satin head wrap, as if she has just woken up. She blocks the camera for a moment with her makeup brush and then reappears, having done her makeup and transformed her dress style into a high-end aesthetic. She then tosses the makeup brush offscreen to the next Black woman, who catches it and follows suit. The makeup brush operates as a metaphorical baton. Asolo's video caught the attention of many other Black women from across the globe and led to the unfolding of what I argue was a cultural moment. This was a transnational cultural moment and cultural shift, but it meant something very distinct among young Black women in South Africa, who were under the hard lockdown at the time.

The Don't Rush Challenge meant something different for us because we have been in crisis. For us, living in what had already been named the rape capital of the world by Interpol, being enslaved by fear of being raped and murdered while living through a pandemic has offered limited opportunity to experience some form of joy. In August 2019, mere months before the March 2020 lockdown, a South African university student named Uyinene Mrwetyana was raped and murdered at a post office in Claremont, South Africa (Lyster 2019). While countless women have suffered the same fate as Mrwetyana, the context within which she was violated exaggerated women's fear of men while confirming the arrogance of hegemonic violent masculinities. Mrwetyana's murder generated national concern, followed by a hashtag movement known as #AmINext, calling men and the state to respond to violence against women. Mrwetyana's murder and the subsequent hashtag activism follow from years of public cases of femicide, such as the 2017 killing of Karabo Mokoena, which led to #RUReferenceList, a movement that exposed perpetrators of violence against women at the university currently known as Rhodes. Cases of rape and femicide have taken up much of our (South African) Black Twitter. Amid the pandemic of violence and the grief that it begets, we must find opportunities to connect and exercise joy. We cannot only be bound by grief. The Don't Rush Challenge was a call to express ourselves in ways other than mourning. And the response to one another's participation was, semhle! You are beautiful.

About a year after the Don't Rush Challenge took hold, I noted that it had become difficult to retrieve the #DontRushChallenge videos on Twitter. Twitter user @Balelekeng tweeted on February 13, 2021, "I saw from that #dontrushchallenge most videos are deleted [for] 'using someone's song for content w/o [without] their permission.'" On February 15, 2021, @itsjessdeb also noted that "Twitter is just suspending all our accounts, you know. . . . [In] hindsight the #dontrushchallenge wasn't a good idea." Consequently, it is now difficult to quote responses to the challenge. However, relying on my own memory and having participated in the challenge myself, I can attest to semhle having been the most common response in South Africa. It also would have been appropriate, since our natural response to beauty is to recognize it as beautiful, and in South Africa, we utilized our own linguistic tools to say so.

Whereas some Don't Rush Challenge videos captured only one individual supposedly "transforming," many videos were done by collectives. Black women's circles of friends, colleagues, and sisters came together, far and wide, to shoot content and edit it into one comprehensive video that showcased the diverse forms of beauty and fashion. This process involved the use and capture of a makeup brush held over the camera lens. After the "great reveal" of one woman, the brush is thrown up or used to transition the attention to the next woman, who supposedly catches the brush and begins her glam process. The kind of commitment and virtual coordination required by a cultural text such as the Don't Rush Challenge is evidence of a feminist community-building project and systems of care, holding one another and celebrating amid chaos. Francesca Sobande and Krys Osei (2020) posit that visual communication, as is exhibited through the Don't Rush Challenge, is a community-based project of self-expression and connection for Black women. By visual communication, they refer to the critical aesthetic and screen depiction of African women's self-expression.

Semhle! Responses to the Book Covers as Outfits Challenge

The Book Covers as Outfits Challenge also demonstrated the making of feminist communities and imaginaries during pandemics. For this challenge, a book cover of one's choice is selected and matched with an outfit similar to the design and feel of the book cover. This is another challenge I participated in, and I thoroughly enjoyed it! While this trend is not new or exclusive to 2020, it certainly became another accessible way to connect with one another in South Africa. It also presented an opportunity to memorialize (primarily Black) authors and their literary contributions through our bodies. For example, in our version of this challenge, my colleagues and I included authors and feminists Pumla Dineo Gqola, Tlaleng Mofokeng, Koleka Putuma, and Zora Neale Hurston. We posted our version of the book covers as outfits challenge on Twitter and on YouTube (including on my channel, Black Girl Chats [2020]) and, where possible, tagged the relevant authors, who retweeted and engaged with our version of the challenge. Notwithstanding the specific cultural moments animated by the Don't Rush Challenge and the Book Covers as Outfits Challenge, there are other examples of how African women exercise bodily autonomy through beauty and self-styling in everyday virtual life.

In a tweet dated May 26, 2020, a Black woman Twitter user, @DJChristySA1, posted a photo of herself in an orange-colored traditional Xhosa culture dress typically worn by women. It is a long dress covering most of her legs, paired with a matching Xhosa head wrap, known as *iqhiya*. Her background is of a farm, which gives the impression that she was under lockdown in a rural area. Black women responded, once again, by pointing out how beautiful she looked. @Mpokie94 commented on the photo and said, "Ye sana it's a pity le lockdown imagine this outfit on those decks, Semhle man," which loosely translates to, "It's a pity the lockdown has us confined because you are so beautiful this outfit deserved to be seen while you play," gesturing to the Twitter user's profession as a music DJ.

On the March 12, 2020, @SiyaBunny tweeted a video of herself wearing different outfits. You see her in a gown, a tracksuit, and pajamas, where she is captured looking comfortable yet very "made-up" and fabulous. She captions the video "Lockdown uniform," to which Black women such as @ZimasaDeti responded, "Semhle Sana. This lockdown has revealed that I don't have enough tracksuits."

@PhindiPhiri tweeted two photos of herself on May 28, 2020. In one image, she is in a yellow dress, and in another, a floral dress, and in both pictures, she stands tall and confidently with her right hand on her hip. @Pearl_Ndlazi responded, "Post-lockdown looks, cuz. Semhle." There are many such engagements among Black women, and a simple search of the term *semhle* will generate the evidence to support this argument.

Toward an African Feminist Perspective of the Don't Rush and Book Covers as Outfits Challenges

African feminisms consider the intersections of gender, race, and imperialism and set out to explore how African women's experiences can be included and narrated in just ways (Lewis 2001). I use an African feminist perspective to understand how the eclectic responses to the pandemic and grief lend themselves to feminist liberatory practices, irrespective of whether the actors self-identify as feminists. In an attempt to demystify and desensationalize feminism (see Ahmed 2017, 21–42), in an African continental context generally and a South African context specifically, it is important to show how feminist work happens in politically oblique and ambiguous ways as well.

In an interview with Elaine Salo, Nigerian British writer Amina Mama (2001) discusses how living a nontraditional life as a girl-woman in society has direct feminist implications even when one is not conscious of them. Mama explains that her entry into feminism was not a conscious process of identifying as an African feminist. Instead, she realized that she embodied her femininity through practices and behaviors typically associated with boyhood and masculinity in the Nigerian context and in Africa more broadly. Studying, being assertive, and taking up space are some of the ways that Mama and (I suspect) many other African women in our contemporary world consciously or unconsciously lend themselves to feminist imaginaries, daring to go beyond where girls and women are encouraged to go. So, while women engaged in media and aesthetic activities like those described in the Don't Rush Challenge and the Book Covers as Outfits Challenge were not doing so to make an active feminist intervention, their participation does have feminist implications. The women engaged in these activities practice bodily autonomy through self-styling, and resistance through fashioning and public body performance. The fact that their participation is also a collective experience is evidence of a sisterhood strengthened by their involvement with digital lifeworlds. It is the feminist imperative to prove that sisterhood is both possible and productive. It is imperative for African feminisms to show African women as complex, not simply as victimized but as creative and regenerative in ways exhibited by women involved in these social media challenges.

Self-Styling, Beauty, and Fashion as Resistance, Agency, and Cocreative Feminist Praxis

Monique Van Vuuren's article "Social Media, Dress, and Body Marking: Exploring Young Women's Imaginative, 'Languages of the Self'" (2018) helps us understand the political and cultural significance of how we adorn our bodies. Van Vuuren offers her concepts of body-talk and bodyhood as a set of everyday practices of resistance through the body in popular and public imaginaries like social media. She is interested in how young women in postapartheid South Africa use their bodies and visual embodiment as radical resistance and a way to claim agency—body, and self. I find her work useful to think alongside as we witness, and in fact are part of, digital communities that facilitate the positive body-talk to which she refers. The Don't Rush Challenge and Book Covers as Outfits Challenge are examples of Van Vuuren's positive body-talk and resistance against shame. When arranged on the body, fashion creates a visual language, provokes responses, stimulates physical interactions, and functions as a form of social identity (Chon 2013). Sarah Nuttal (2009, 108–30) refers to Michel Foucault's definition of self-styling or self-stylization as a technology of the self. Technologies of the self are how we relate to and operate on our bodies, thoughts, and conduct to transform ourselves. Nuttal highlights how Foucault's technologies of the self explore political liberation and expressions of freedom through bodily life. Through self-styling, we are creatively, knowingly, and unknowingly involved in the process of producing and consuming knowledge about the world and ourselves.

The politics of beauty and fashion are complex and interwoven with imperialist histories and experiences, especially in the African context, as Simidele Dosekun (2016) points out. We know who and what is considered beautiful for women; African women, particularly, have historical and sociocultural implications. We also know that African women's bodily choices have been limited through essentialist ideas of Africa and African women and that they remain policed even in contemporary society. The politics of respectability, which are manifested in and across many African cultures and traditions, continue to shame aesthetically defiant or deviant women, among many other types of transgressions. The boundaries of respectability are gendered and entangled with the body, and with how it is dressed and moves in space (Hungwu 2006). The history of control over women's access to the public sphere, bodily freedom, and style of dress is consistent and steadfast across the African continent. Evelyn Lutwama-Rukundo (2016) describes sexually provocative outfits and asserts that skimpy aesthetics encourage assumptions about the sexuality of the women who wear them. Black women, through the Don't Rush Challenge and their everyday digital archiving of their self-styling—where they celebrate various forms of style, particularly skimpy fashion—are engaged in a rebellious act against a context in which so many of our choices are policed.

The proliferation of semhle as a response to a transnational call of bodily autonomy has feminist implications because it speaks to the deliberate formulation of communities and sisterhood. This sisterhood recognizes oneself in the other and intentionally celebrates our choices regarding how we reveal or conceal our bodies. It is important to note that while wearing "skimpy" fashion is an obvious transgression in this context, even being fully clothed can be a productive transgression. By this, I mean that semhle, as a cultural and linguistic coding practice in the virtual, has indicated that the ideas of beauty among (primarily young) African women are not limited to one aesthetic but rather draw from diverse, heterogeneous expressions of fashion and beauty. Beauty is everywhere. It is in all of us.

However, I am also, perhaps reluctantly, suspicious of the upward mobility of Black women's languages of self through social media and under the specific conditions of a hard lockdown. I wonder whether these trends and challenges we participate in, willingly and so freely, can occur as freely and willingly in our offline, in-person worlds? Given South Africa's status as the rape capital of the world and the current pandemic of gender-based violence and femicide, I wonder whether our willingness to show up in the ways we do online, aesthetically but also as fully agentic, powerful, and confident in our bodies, is an impossibility in our offline contexts. While I contest rape myths associated with our forms of dress, we cannot deny that how we dress is often used against us to justify the violence enacted on us. The corrective nature of gender-based violence is also related to our claim to bodily autonomy and integrity. The more we show up as belonging to ourselves, the more violent masculinities work to "correct" us into docility and fear. These are the mechanics of patriarchy. While I am attentive to our forms of agency and community building, I also urge us to think critically about why the transference of our bodily autonomy does not easily hold in our otherwise offline worlds. How might we extend this positive body-talk to the very contexts we find ourselves in, without fear or the risk of being violated?

Sbwl: The Labor of Love and Care Work

Many people in South Africa, our friends, and our family gained weight under the hard lockdown. I know I certainly did! Twitter user @AfikileDube can also attest to weight gain attributed to the lockdown because she tweeted photos of herself on August 10, 2020, with the caption "New body, who dis? #Lockdownweightgain." Food and the general labor of home work or care work certainly became a matter of public interest and spectacle most curated online. One could speculate that most of the increase in our cooking and eating habits may have resulted from COVID-19 anxiety, otherwise known as stress eating. But it is most likely that we experimented more in the kitchen to fill up our time, and because we seldom have time to cook cuisines outside of what we know and are used to. As a result of the closure of restaurants under the hard lockdown in South Africa, many of us (of course, middle-class) people missed some of our favorite restaurants and fast-food treats. This could only result in one thing: cravings and the labor of making our homemade versions. To crave, desire, and long for something in the Xhosa language is *u-sabawela*. Social media users, particularly those of us on Black Twitter, have colloquialized and shortened *u-sabawela* to *sbwl*, which has been appropriated across diverse language and cultural groups of Black people in South Africa. Around the second half of 2019, sbwl emerged on social media, but some Twitter users were still unsure what it meant. Twitter user @busiswah offered a definition of sbwl on September 4, 2020, when she tweeted, "What does sbwl mean" and attached a screenshot with a definition that reads as follows: "The phrase 'sbwl' is a local slang term from the Xhosa language, originating from the word 'sabaweli' meaning crave, desire, yearn or want and is normally used for things one cannot have."

Online Responses to Black Women's Labor of Cooking

On April 17, 2020, during lockdown level 5, South African celebrity food influencer and cook Neo Nontso (@NeoNontso) posted images of her version of Kentucky Fried Chicken's popular streetwise meal, which comprises one or more pieces of fried chicken and fries. Nontso posted these images on Twitter, where many of the responses were "Sbwl" (expressing a craving for the food) and "Sbwl the recipe," which she then posted and shared on her Instagram. An even larger number of Twitter users responded to her Twitter photos by saying her version looked and possibly tasted better than that of the franchise itself. Nontso also shared many other recipes, including hot wings and donuts. As a well-known and talented food influencer and cook, Nontso has been asked on Twitter and on numerous occasions to remake other fast-food and beverage favorites such as McDonald's selections and even beer. On many occasions, she has responded positively to these requests and invested in the labor of love involved in cooking and sharing.

On May 2, 2020, under lockdown level 4, another popular food influencer and cook, Luyanda Mafanya (@Luyanda_Maf), who often tweets under her hashtag #cookingwithLuyanda, gave her time to Twitter users. She tweeted, "I'm up, I have time. Ask me any cooking questions that you have, things you struggle with within the kitchen, or you could let me know what you'd wanna learn (I'll answer to the best of my ability)." That tweet received most of its engagement from Black women who *sbwl* to learn various things related to food and cooking. They asked Luyanda to advise them on recipes for making pasta sauces, prawn curry, pork and lamb shank, buns, and the lockdown favorite in South Africa, banana bread. These are not the foods one would typically prepare on an ordinary Wednesday night in their home. We wanted to learn how to prepare the extravagant treats that we would usually go out for as part of a fine dining experience. Many other Black women asked Luyanda for advice on which nonstick pots to purchase and what kitchen appliances, utensils, and spices they should invest in for better cooking proficiency.

Besides well-known food/cooking celebrities like Nontso and Mafanya, other Black women also found their way into the hearts of food lovers. On Twitter, Lwazi Khoza, otherwise known as Mfaz'Omnyama (@mfazomnyama_), rose to the occasion with what appeared to be delicious food preparation tips and recipes. Many of my friends also invested their time and energy in preparing food in their kitchens. I, too, have been influenced and encouraged to nurture my body in my kitchen while sharing with friends and family what the meal of the day was. It is clear that while we could not typically gather and break bread together due to the pandemic, we remained connected through the virtual gastro-economics of food.

African Feminist Considerations with Care Work Such as Cooking

The gendered nature of care work results from the social construction of gender itself. To attain metaphorical and symbolic certificates in masculinity or femininity, specific gender performances, mannerisms, and even forms of dress are encouraged. Traditional femininity is expected to engage in activities that give service and labor without recognition or remuneration. Child-rearing and caring, cooking, and cleaning are examples of the care work or home work I refer to. How do these relate to an African feminist framework? According to African feminist scholar Ifi Amadiume (1987), while Western feminism and anthropology contest the domestic labor associated with femininity, this perspective fails to recognize the social and cultural context within which African women find ourselves.

Amadiume further argues that Western feminism tends to have a colonizing effect on African feminism and our relationship with femininity and gender performance. Historically, she writes, home work and care work were considered honorable responsibilities for women and not placed in a binary that articulated traditional or "domesticated" femininities as powerless and docile compared to "militant," undomesticated, or nontraditional femininities. The African feminist perspective further complicates binaries by highlighting how African women were also queens and matriarchs of queendoms and actively engaged in challenging colonialists strategically and militarily (Farrar 1997). This is especially true of the Dahomey women warriors in West Africa during the nineteenth century. Showing how African femininities emerge and are embodied in their multiplicity and adaptability to what is needed, we can make sense of how African women may enjoy being in the kitchen, cooking, connecting, and sharing as much as we may enjoy being warriors and workers in other ways.

Desiree Lewis (2001) reminds us that while African feminism may have been more consciously theorized in response to Western feminism's limited portrayal of African and other Third World women's experiences, it has also (and probably most importantly) developed as more goal oriented and proactive. This means that African feminism is invested in the process of inspiring women to be active agents in the cocreation of their—our—lives, even if their doing so may go against the traditional social and cultural scripting of femininities in African contexts or even subvert the essentialist claims made by Western feminism. In relation to African feminism, Glory Joy Gatwiri (2016, 267) asserts that "my definition of African feminism is that it is a school of thought and mode of discourse that attempts to understand the multiple complexities and challenges presented by sexism—a derivative of patriarchy, poverty, and at times colonization—faced by the African woman. This African feminist approach is one that makes an attempt to educate, empower and elevate women to a position where they can own their power not against men but alongside them."

So, while there is always a disproportionate amount of work involved for women in the home, especially in nuclear family structures where the feminization of domestic work is emphasized, there is also another narrative. We have the opportunity to engage African feminism as subverting patriarchal ideologies while also claiming autonomy on its own terms and outside of a Western lens that may render cooking, for example, oppressive patriarchal work. Not all African women need saving. Many things can be true at once. It can be true that the compulsory domestication of girlhood and womanhood is discriminatory and problematic. But it can also be true that we have opportunities to connect and be of service to ourselves. Arlene Voski Avakian and Barbara Harber (2005) argue that while feminist studies has paid attention to housework and domesticity as patriarchal oppression, it has neglected to fully consider women's complex and varied relationship with food and cooking. Avakian and Harber further note that cooking can be a source of creative expression and community. Much like the rich conversation and exchange of knowledge that occurs when Black women gather to peel vegetables and cook the slaughtered meat of a goat or cow on a black three-legged pot, known as the *drie-foot*, African pot, ahead of a funeral or wedding, there is community and the possibility of pleasure.

Black women's political, social, and cultural authority in the kitchen is often undermined because of the incessant and problematic stereotype of women as naturally "good cooks," as Kimberly D. Nettles-Barcelón and colleagues (2015) note. When Black women are seen as "natural" custodians of the kitchen, their investment in our food cultures goes un- or underacknowledged, and they are relegated to a normative cuisine known as soul food in the American context, or "seven colors" in South Africa. But we do not have one "culinary trail," Nettles-Barcelón and colleagues argue. This is evidenced by the diverse foods prepared and recipes shared online by African women. The diverse "food voices" of African women assert our culinary skills and our social, political, and cultural connections with one another in our capacity as food laborers. Furthermore, the longing to be in the presence of loved ones, to sbwl, together with our sharing of food and recipes online, undoes a supposedly oppressive thing by turning it into a pleasurable and community-building exercise.

Conclusion

Black women have shown that we exist in multiple, complex, and contradictory ways. Even in otherwise violent and oppressive contexts, there are opportunities to exist in agentic and eclectic ways. While some perceive the conditions for femininity as unfavorable and unjust, there are re-creative possibilities within which we engage to form bonds of community and joy. We—those of us with access to the favorable side of the digital divide—have also demonstrated that beyond the biological materiality of our bodies, we can extend ourselves into alternative forms for purposes of connection and community building. Through our media activity, aesthetic practices, fashioning, and care work, we show the possibilities of feminist world-making practices that are supported by connection and community building. While I am not romanticizing being Black, African, and woman, I also refuse to only think about and navigate the world from a downtrodden positionality. We are here. We are alive. We are taking up space. We are taking up arms of courage, love, and community even amid chaos and grief.

Semhle. Beautiful. I see you. Sbwl. We long for pleasure.

Notes

1. The chapter title, "Semhle, Sbwl," invokes Xhosa colloquial words developed and used mainly on social media (specifically Twitter) by Black South Africans. Semhle means "You are beautiful," and Sbwl means "craving."

2. Consent is ambiguous in social media research. However, I consider that social media participation is public in nature. Our interactions and posts are for public consumption, save for instances in which users have locked some accounts. If one tweets under a hashtag, I argue that the tweeted content may be disseminated and used publicly since the hashtag is also a public archival tool (Bonilla and Rosa 2015).

References

Ahlawat, Jyoti. 2020. "How Social Media Has Become a Site for Sisterhood in the COVID-19 Pandemic." *Feminism in India* (blog), July 1, 2020. https://feminisminindia.com/2020/07/01/social-media-safe-space-for-women-sisterhood-covid-19/.

Ahmed, Sara. 2017. *Living a Feminist Life*. Durham, N.C.: Duke University Press.

Amadiume, Ifi. 1987. *Male Daughters, Female Husbands: Gender and Sex in an African Society*. London: Zed Books.

Avakian, Arlene Voski, and Harber, Barbara. 2005. *From Betty Crocker to Feminist Food Studies: Critical Perspectives on Women and Food*. Amherst: University of Massachusetts Press.

Baer, Hester. 2016. "Redoing Feminism: Digital Activism, Body Politics, and Neoliberalism." *Feminist Media Studies* 16 (1): 17–34.

Black Girl Chats. 2020. "Book Covers as Outfits Challenge!" Uploaded April 12, 2020. YouTube video, 1:45. https://www.youtube.com/watch?v=JWRcE-uU2gk.

Bonilla, Yarimar, and Jonathan Rosa. 2015. "#Ferguson: Digital Protest, Hashtag Ethnography, and the Racial Politics of Social Media in the United States." *Journal of the American Ethnological Society* 42 (1): 4–17.

Brock, André, Jr. 2020. *Distributed Blackness: African American Cybercultures.* New York: New York University Press.

Brown-Luthando, Mercy. 2020. "South Africa's 2nd Pandemic: Reflecting on Gender-Based Violence During and Beyond COVID-19." AIDC: Alternative Information & Development Centre. September 10, 2020. https://aidc.org.za /south-africas-2nd-pandemic-reflecting-on-gender-based-violence-during -and-beyond-covid-19/.

Chiumbu, Sarah Helen, and Dina Ligaga. 2013. "'Communities of Stranger-hoods?': Internet, Mobile Phones and the Changing Nature of Radio Cultures in South Africa." *Telematics and Informatics* 30 (3): 242–51.

Chon, Harah. 2013. "Fashion as Aesthetic Experience: A Discussion of Subject-Object Interaction." Paper presented at the Fifth International Congress of International Association of Societies of Design Research, Shibaura Institute of Technology, Japan, August 2013. Research Gate. Uploaded August 2013. https://www.researchgate.net/publication/268010781.

Clark, Meredith D. 2018. "#BlackTwitter." *Medium*, February 26, 2018. https:// medium.com/informed-and-engaged/black-twitter-9a95550773c8.

Clough, Patricia T. 2008. "The Affective Turn: Political Economy, Biomedia and Bodies." *Theory, Culture and Society* 25 (1): 1–22.

Dosekun, Simidele. 2016. "The Politics of Fashion and Beauty in Africa." *Feminist Africa* 21: 1–6.

Farrar, Tarikhu. 1997. "The Queenmother, Matriarchy, and the Question of Female Political Authority in Precolonial West African Monarchy." *Journal of Black Studies* 27 (5): 579–97.

Gatwiri, Glory Joy, with Helen Jaqueline McLaren. 2016. "Discovering My Own African Feminism: Embarking on a Journey to Explore Kenya Women's Oppression." *Journal of International Women's Studies* 17 (4): 263–73.

Hungwe, Chipo. 2006. "Putting Them in Their Place: 'Respectable' and 'Unrespectable' Women in Zimbabwean Gender Struggles." *Feminist Africa*, no. 6, 33–47.

Isama, Antoinette. 2020. "The Real Reason the #DontRushChallenge Was Created." *Teen Vogue*, April 7, 2020. https://www.teenvogue.com/story/dont -rush-challenge-creator.

Lewis, Desiree. 2001. "Introduction: African Feminisms." *Agenda: Empowering Women for Gender Equity*, no. 50, 4–10.

Lutwama-Rukundo, Evelyn. 2016. "Skimpy Fashion and Sexuality in Sheebah Karungi's Performances." *Feminist Africa* 21: 52–62.

Lyster, Rosa. 2019. "The Death of Uyinene Mrwetyana and the Rise of South Africa's 'Am I Next?' Movement." *New Yorker*, September 12, 2019.

Malik, Aqdas, Cassandra Heyman-Schrum, and Aditya Johri. 2019. "Use of Twitter Across Educational Settings: A Review of the Literature." *International Journal of Educational Technology in Higher Education* 16: article 36. https://doi.org/10.1186/s41239-019-0166-x.

Mama, Amina. 2001. "Talking About Feminism in Africa." Interview by Elaine Salo. *Agenda: Empowering Women for Gender Equity*, no. 50, 58–63.

Mazibuko, Mbali. 2020. "Under the Eyes of COVID-19: Grief and Otherness." *Daily Vox News*, May 11, 2020. https://www.thedailyvox.co.za/under-the -eyes-of-covid-19-grief-and-otherness/.

McDonald, Soraya Nadia. 2014. "Black Twitter: A Virtual Community Ready to Hashtag Out a Response to Cultural Issues." *Washington Post*, January 20, 2014.

Nettles-Barcelón, Kimberly D., Gillian Clark, Courtney Thorsson, Jessica Kenyatta Walker, and Psyche Williams-Forson. 2015. "Black Women's Food Work as Critical Space." *Gastronomica* 15 (4): 34–49.

Nuttall, Sarah. 2009. *Entanglement: Literary and Cultural Reflections on Post-Apartheid*. Johannesburg: Wits University Press.

Ramafoko, Lebogang. 2020. "Gender-Based Violence: What Does 16 Days of Activism Mean When Women Are Still Dying?" *Mail and Guardian* (Johannesburg), December 6, 2020.

Sobande, Francesca, and Krys Osei. 2020. "*An African City*: Black Women's Creativity, Pleasure, Diasporic (Dis)Connections and Resistance Through Aesthetic and Media Practices and Scholarship." *Communication, Culture and Critique* 13 (2): 204–21.

South African Government News Agency. 2021. "President Launches Fund to Respond to Gender-Based Violence." February 5, 2021. https://www.sanews .gov.za/south-africa/president-launches-fund-respond-gender-based -violence.

Van Vuuren, Monique. 2018. "Social Media, Dress, and Body Marking: Exploring Young Women's Imaginative, 'Languages of the Self.'" *Agenda: Empowering Women for Gender Equity* 32 (3): 21–38.

Yang, Guobin, and Rosemary Clark. 2015. "Social Media and Time." *Social Media + Society*, April–June 2015. https://doi.org/10.1177/2056305115578144.

Zikalala, Zukolwenkosi. 2016. "Black Queers Must Play." Honors research report, Wits University. In author's possession.

Our Ethic of Care

On Doing Black Feminist Work When You Listen to the Ancestors

Julia S. Jordan-Zachery

Dear [Name]

Thank you for your abstract proposal. Based on your proposal [title], I would like to invite you to submit to the volume "Black Women and 'Rona." This invitation does not guarantee that your submission will be included in the book. After submission, it will go through an initial review.

As part of compiling this edited volume, I offer this ethic of care. I want to center the humanity of Black femmes, girls, and women in this writing and, as such, was compelled to think through how to approach this project critically.

Working in Community

In part, I came to this project because Black women often heal in community. To honor that, I thought it would be important to organize small writing groups consisting of three authors (or three teams). Much of the academy is set up around individualism. As a way of countering this, I'm willing to help organize small writing/working groups. You have to opt into this by emailing me (July 3, 2020). These writing groups are designed to help you sustain your project.

Time of Submission

Your submission is due on/or before November 13, 2020, at 4 p.m. EST. Please communicate with me if you need to deviate from this time frame. The goal is to have a solid working project by January 2021. This means that I will conduct an initial review and, if needed, engage with you about ways to strengthen your submission. Once you receive my response, you will have three weeks to engage any edits, etc., and return the submission. My goal is to foster open and engaged communication with you. But I can't do it alone. So, I ask you to please be in dialogue with me as this project unfolds.

Submission Checklist

The Cover Page
___ Title
___ Name
___ Contact Information
___ Abstract (150–200 words)

Engaging Our Stories About Black Women

As we write, I want us to think carefully and critically about how we describe and offer details on Black femmes, girls, and women. Language matters. So, for example, are you using a language that suggests that Black femmes, girls, and women are broken and in need of fixing? In this volume, we want to tell the truth about Black femmes, girls, and women, *and* we also want to be mindful of not perpetuating existing narratives and tropes.

___ I am mindful of not perpetuating existing harmful narratives and tropes.

Black as a Racial Group

___ I capitalized Black when referring to the racial group.

Conscientious Engagement with Literature (primarily for those
working on academic/scholarly papers)

___ I cited Black women. Please cite Black women!

___ I actively engaged with the scholarship of Black women and not
simply just referenced their name.

___ I cited a junior faculty member.

___ I cited myself, if appropriate.

___ I moved beyond the canon to include at least one "fresh" name.

Note on Proofreading

___ Have I proofread my submission?

   Suggestions on how to proofread

      a. Have someone read it for you.

      b. Read the last sentence first and work backward.

      c. Read it out loud.

      d. Record it as you read and then listen to it—a few days later.

      e. Give yourself time to think, write, and then edit.

___ I accepted changes.

___ I turned off track changes.

___ I used Times New Roman, 12 point font.

___ I followed the formatting of the Chicago Manual of Style (for
those writing academic/scholarly papers).

___ I have page numbers, and they are positioned in the top right
corner.

___ I spelled out acronyms the first time I used them.

___ I checked for passive voice. A corny, but a good way to check
for passive voice—use "by zombies" (see the National Archives'
guide to "Passive Voice and Zombies," https://www.archives.gov
/open/plain-writing/tips/passive-voice.html).

___ Did I overuse -ly words? Often words ending in -ly are not needed. So, do the -ly check and delete where necessary.

___ Did I double-space?

___ I wrote no more than 20 pages, double spaced, and including references (for those writing academic/scholarly papers).

___ I wrote no more than 2,500 words, double spaced (for those writing prose/poetry, etc.).

___ I spell-checked and checked the vocabulary.

Citations (for those writing academic/scholarly papers)

___ I used the *Chicago Manual of Style*.

___ I cited myself.

___ All citations follow the in-text method (no use of footnotes/ endnotes for citations).

___ All endnotes/footnotes are placed at the end of the document.

The Nitty-Gritty of Writing

___ I wrote my introduction last to ensure that it truly captures what I'm writing about.

___ My title fits well with my chapter. It is short and to the point.

___ I highlighted, in the introduction, what this chapter is about. Is it easily identifiable?

___ I explained to the reader why this paper is important, what gap it is filling, and what its central contribution is, and it is all easily identifiable in the introduction.

___ I did not just end the paper; I have a substantive conclusion.

___ I checked to determine that I have topic sentences in each paragraph.

___ I checked my transitions between and within paragraphs.

___ Jargon, I minimized my use of jargon.

___ I wrote in an accessible manner for folks outside of my discipline or even the academy.

___ I wrote in a manner that is clear, concise, and to the point.

___ My submission fits the call for chapters.

Methods, Data, Tables, Figures, Images, and Appendices

___ I have clearly and succinctly articulated how I'm doing what I'm doing. That is, my method/approach is clearly articulated and can be followed by others outside of the discipline.

___ I have concisely shown who is involved or what is involved to help me make my argument. My data are clear.

___ My tables and figures are referenced and explained in text and are clearly labeled.

___ All images are referenced and explained in the text, and the image is clearly and visibly replicated in the submission.

___ I've attached my appendices.

Permissions Are Key

___ I have permission to cite/reuse previously published works. I have included this along with my submission.

___ IRB permission, do I need it? I include evidence that I have it.

Original Submission

___ I am sure that this is an original submission and that it is not currently published or under review with another entity.

In Community, We Submit This Project Together

___ I have recommended at least one reviewer of this edited volume.

Submission

___ I submitted my chapter as a Word document!

Congratulations. Now let's celebrate what we have created together.

CONTRIBUTORS

Tamaya Bailey is a social worker based in Dallas, Texas, and has interests in mental health, substance abuse prevention and treatment, and treatment for individuals living with chronic illness. She earned a master's in social work with a concentration in mental health and substance abuse from the University of Texas at Arlington. She is a proud U.S. Air Force veteran.

reelaviolette botts-ward is a doctoral candidate in the African Diaspora Studies program at the University of California, Berkeley. Her research is on Black women's healing spaces, and she looks at the ways in which embodied, ancestral, spiritual, and creative healing occurs within and beyond the physical landscape of home. She is deeply passionate about using her research as a model for healing in the everyday lives of Black women within and beyond the academy. She merges her poetry with her theoretical interventions to produce work that speaks to the range of affective experiences Black women are taught to be silent about. Her first book, *mourning my inner[black/girl]child*, was published with Nomadic Press in 2021. In her role as founder and CEO of #BlackWomxnHealing, she works closely with the California Black Women's Health Project and Flourish Agenda to provide sister circle–style retreat opportunities for Black women across California.

Kyrah K. Brown is an assistant professor of public health and director of the Maternal Health Equity Research Lab at the University of Texas at Arlington. Her research focuses on the social and structural factors that shape the health and birth outcomes of Black women across the life course. Her work centers the voices and experiences of Black women to inform policy and interventions aimed at achieving health equity, including birth equity. She has emerging work focused on COVID-19-related knowledge, perceptions, facilitators, and barriers among pregnant and recently pregnant Black women.

Brianna Y. Clark serves as a resident family medicine physician in North Carolina. Her special interests are rural medicine, primary care, and reproductive health. Dr. Clark is passionate about providing medical access to underserved communities across the Southeast. Dr. Clark received her doctorate of osteopathic medicine from the Edward Via College of Osteopathic Medicine, Carolinas Campus. She received her master's in public health and a graduate certificate in nonprofit management from Texas A&M University School of Public Health and the Bush School of Government and Public Service. She received a bachelor of science from Baylor University in biology, and she is a proud AmeriCorps Community HealthCorps alumna.

Kenyatta Dawson is the director of the Office of Undergraduate Research in the Division of the Vice President for Research and adjunct assistant professor for management at the University of Texas at Arlington. Dr. Dawson's research interests include (1) mentorship and advising of adult learners in higher education, (2) adult learning methods and staff/faculty professional development in higher education, and (3) social justice– and equity-oriented leaders/leadership preparation and continuance. Collectively, her research interests and current projects highlight data-driven discovery regarding technology, influences in access/equity, and health and the human condition.

In her professional capacity she specializes in academic affairs, undergraduate research, student success, and inclusive student retention and completion efforts (diversity, equity, and inclusion).

LeConté J. Dill is a community-accountable scholar, educator, and poet born and raised in South Central Los Angeles. In her work, she listens to and shows up for urban Black girls and rigorously documents their experiences of safety, resilience, resistance, and wellness. For nearly a decade, she served on the faculty at several schools and programs of public health across the United States. Currently, Dr. Dill is an associate professor of African American and African studies at Michigan State University and a research associate at the African Centre for Migration & Society at Wits University in Johannesburg, South Africa. Dr. Dill's scholarly and creative works have been published in a diverse array of spaces, such as the *Du Bois Review, Journal of Adolescent Research, Journal of Poetry Therapy, Poetry Magazine, Mom Egg Review*, and *Feminist Wire*.

Maryam O. Funmilayo is a public health nutrition educator and researcher, as well as a Ronin Institute research scholar. She earned her bachelor's degree in human nutrition from Kansas State University, her master of arts degree in health education from East Carolina University, and her master of public health degree with a concentration in health disparities from Lamar University. Her professional and research expertise include faith-based nutrition education and health promotion, community-based participatory research with immigrant and refugee female populations, community advocacy, community organization, food literacy, women's health, and global health. Her lived experiences in Nigeria, Canada, the United States, Egypt, and Ghana have fueled her passion to research the role that nutrition education and health promotion play in women's health, especially among women of African descent suffering from breast cancer, diabetes, heart disease, and uterine fibroids. Her passion for cross-cultural engagement has led her to utilize ethnography and the PEN-3 model as a fieldwork approach and a health promotion tool, respectively. She enjoys reading, freelance writing, grant writing, mentoring, traveling, volunteering, learning different languages, and spending quality time with her family and friends.

Brandie Green is a clinical assistant professor in the Department of Kinesiology at the University of Texas at Arlington. Dr. Green has expertise in maternal and child health and health disparities, and she teaches courses related to marginalized populations. Dr. Green has had the opportunity to work in the field of public health for several nonprofit organizations with the overarching goal of reducing health disparities and improving access to quality health care. She also has experience in health-care administration, workforce development, and grant writing. Dr. Green's research and teaching focuses on improving health-care resources for minority populations and underserved communities, especially in the maternal and child health realm. She holds a bachelor of science in biology from Xavier University of Louisiana, a master's in public health from the University of North Texas Health Science Center, and a doctoral degree in public and urban administration and policy from the University of Texas at Arlington.

Courtney Jackson is the coordinator in the Department of Kinesiology of the College of Nursing and Health Innovation at the University of Texas at Arlington (UTA) and loves working with college students. She has spent most of her career in the education industry, gaining experience in advising and student development. While advising for UTA's Exercise Science and Public Health program and being an academic coach for the Accelerate Online Public Health program are her primary pursuits by day, Courtney also enjoys reading, traveling, volunteering, spending time with family and friends, mentoring young women of color, and serving in her beloved sorority, Delta Sigma Theta Sorority. She has a bachelor of science in business administration with an emphasis in finance from the University of South Alabama and a master of education with an emphasis in counseling and student affairs from Texas A&M University–Commerce.

Sara Jean-Francois is a candidate in the Master's in Public Policy program at the Brandeis Heller School for Social Policy, and a health policy and management graduate from Providence College. Her research focuses on systemic issues that affect communities of color today.

Julia S. Jordan-Zachery is a professor in and chair of the Women's, Gender, and Sexuality Studies Department at Wake Forest University. She has written a number of articles and several books, including the award-winning *Black Women, Cultural Images and Social Policy*. She is the co-editor of *Black Girl Magic Beyond the Hashtag* and *Black Women and da 'Rona*. She has also produced the documentary *Healing Roots* and a poetry book, *Eat the Meat and Spit Out the Bones*.

Angela K. Lewis-Maddox is professor of political science at the University of Alabama at Birmingham and former interim department chair and program director. She is the author of *Conservatism in the Black Community: To the Right and Misunderstood*, and her work appears in *College Teaching, National Political Science Review, PS: Political Science & Politics*, and *Polity*.

Annet Matebwe was born and raised in Bulawayo, Zimbabwe, and relocated to the United Kingdom for work. She now works as a commercial lawyer in London. She studied law at the University of KwaZulu-Natal in South Africa and went on to pursue two master's degrees at the University of the Western Cape in conjunction with Humboldt University of Berlin and the University of Law in the United Kingdom. Annet is the first of three children and the first to go to university in her family. When she is not working, Annet enjoys writing, which not only offers her a creative outlet to share her thoughts but also serves as a form of advocacy, her way of bringing light to causes that matter to her.

Mbali Mazibuko is a Wits University graduate, having received a bachelor of arts with joint honors in sociology and political sciences (cum laude) and master of arts in sociology. Her provocations are rooted in affect theories and feminist ethics of love, care, and rage. A methodological ethic of feminist rage is what holds her work, informing how she interacts with scholarship and how she develops her own scholarship. She is also cofounder of a Black feminist platform and collective, Black Girl Chats. The platform is committed to unpacking complex and layered issues pertaining to gender and the various ways in which it intersects with other axes of difference in the South African context. She is a feminist badass, frustrating the very boundaries of what is considered acceptable and unacceptable. She has a deep love for students and pedagogical justice. She is currently a PhD candidate in women's and gender studies, under the supervision of Prof. Tamara Shefer and Dr. Sisa Ngabaza at the University of the Western Cape, South Africa.

Radscheda Nobles is an assistant professor in the Department of History, Politics and Social Justice at Winston-Salem State University. She earned her doctorate in sociology from Howard University, her master's in criminal justice from Fayetteville State University, and her bachelor's in criminal justice from Shaw University. Her current research explores the impact of criminal justice policies and practices on marginalized populations.

Nimot Ogunfemi is a Nigerian-American arts-based researcher and healer in training. She is a doctoral student in counseling psychology at the University of Illinois Urbana-Champaign. She utilizes art-based inquiry in her research as a tool toward decolonization and global equity. She has developed collective arts-based research and healing activities aimed at self-reflection and meaning making. As a community healer, she has facilitated transgender, bisexual, and Black graduate student support groups. Her research interests are at the intersection of diasporic spiritual well-being and social justice.

J. Mercy Okaalet is an infectious disease epidemiologist in Fort Worth, Texas. She holds a bachelor of science from John Brown University and received her master of public health in epidemiology from the University of North Texas Health Science Center. Her major initiatives as an epidemiologist have been in the area of disease surveillance, with a focus in infectious disease investigation and control, outbreak management and mitigation, and health-care-acquired infections. Her response efforts have focused on an array of organisms and conditions including murine typhus, Legionella, West Nile fever, multidrug-resistant organisms, and vaccine-preventable disease outbreaks. Additionally, she has advanced knowledge and experience in public health emergency preparedness, particularly in the planning and implementation of critical measures for disaster prevention, management, and response. She has actively provided guidance for Homeland Security's BioWatch program (an early detection system for airborne bioterrorism attacks), high consequence infectious disease preparations and monitoring, and training and planning for a potential radiation event at local nuclear power plant.

Chizoba Uzoamaka Okoroma is a graduate of the University of Texas at Arlington with a bachelor of science in public health. She is passionate about global health and maternal and child health. She is planning to pursue her master of public health in epidemiology to prepare for a career in providing health education and advocacy to help improve the health and well-being of vulnerable populations.

Peace Ossom-Williamson, MLS, MS, and AHIP, is associate director of the National Center for Data Services of the Network of the National Library of Medicine, located at the New York University Health Sciences Library. She is a medical librarian and health educator with experience providing data services, scholarly communications, and outreach in libraries. She is a recognized researcher, receiving the 2021 Texas Woman's University Hallmark Alumni Award and the Ida and George Eliot Prize from the Medical Library Association for a co-authored article of hers deemed most effective in furthering medical librarianship in 2020. As an active educator, she teaches research data services in libraries at San José State University and public health informatics at the University of Texas at Arlington.

Elizabeth Peart is a ten-year-old writer, playwright, illustrator, and actor. She has written several books that take up themes of fantasy and science fiction, two of which are published. Her dream is to create worlds that reflect her image and ideas, and that people like her can relate to.

INDEX

Women of Irmandande da Boa Morte
  (Sisterhood of the Good Death), 95
Woodson, Jaqueline, *Brown Girl Dreaming*, 192
world-making, 194–95, 212–13
writing, 6–7, 8, 43–44, 58, 73n7, 106, 119–20, 130, 181, 185–86

Xhosa, 195, 198–99, 203, 207–8, 213n1

Yahya-Othman, Saida, 103–4
Yalom, Irvin D., 112n2
Yang, Guobin, 197

yoga, 95, 106–7, 128–29
Yoruba, 96, 103–4, 131
Young, Daniel, 18
youth, 51–52, 74n11, 75n17. *See also* Black
  girlhood
YouTube, 95–96, 106–7, 202. *See also*
  social media

Zangewa, Billie, 107–8
Zikalala, Zukolwenkosi, 199
Zoom, 45–47, 57–58, 60–63, 73n5, 133–34, 155–57. *See also* virtual